THE PHILOSOPHY OF
FRANCIS BACON

THE PHILOSOPHY OF
FRANCIS BACON

AN ESSAY ON ITS DEVELOPMENT
FROM 1603 TO 1609
WITH NEW TRANSLATIONS OF
FUNDAMENTAL TEXTS

by Benjamin Farrington

Phoenix Books

THE UNIVERSITY OF CHICAGO PRESS

THE UNIVERSITY OF CHICAGO PRESS, CHICAGO 60637
Liverpool University Press, Liverpool 7, England
The University of Toronto Press, Toronto 5, Canada

To my friend

DOROTHEA WALEY SINGER

CONTENTS

PART ONE: INTRODUCTION

1. Bacon hopes to effect his reforms administratively   11
2. First attempts at a literary presentation of his plan   16
3. Out with Aristotle and in with the Bible   21
4. From the imitation of nature to domination over nature   27
5. The ethical optimism of Bacon   30
6. The upgrading of the manual arts   32
7. Mistaken tactics of *The Masculine Birth of Time*   35
8. Bacon rethinks his position. The sociology of knowledge   38
9. Thoughts and Conclusions, Refutation of Philosophies   45
10. Magic, Alchemy and Modern Science   51

PART TWO: TRANSLATIONS

The Masculine Birth of Time   59
Thoughts and Conclusions   73
The Refutation of Philosophies   103
BIBLIOGRAPHY   134
INDEX   137

All references to Bacon's text are to the collected edition of Spedding, Ellis and Heath, 14 vols. London 1857–74. The abbreviation Sp. is used for this edition. If the original is in Latin the first reference is to the Latin, the second (in brackets) to the translation. But I have everywhere assumed the liberty to alter this translation or make a completely new one.

My heaviest debt to a contemporary writer is to Professor Paolo Rossi of Milan. His writings bearing closely on the subject of my work are listed elsewhere (p. 21). But all my references to him are to the most comprehensive of his Baconian studies, *Francesco Bacone: Dalla Magia alla Scienza*. Bari, 1957.

PART ONE

INTRODUCTION

*I would address one general admonition to all, that they con-
sider what are the true ends of knowledge, and that they seek
it neither for pleasure of the mind, nor for contention, nor for
superiority over others, nor for profit, nor fame, nor power, nor
for any of these inferior things; but for the benefit and use of
life; and that they perfect and govern it in charity. For it was
from lust of power that the angels fell, from lust of knowledge
that men fell; but of charity there can be no excess, neither
did angel or man ever come in danger by it.*

*Of myself I wish to say nothing. But in respect of the busi-
ness which is in hand I entreat men to believe that it is not an
opinion to be held, but* A WORK TO BE DONE; *and to be
well assured that I am labouring to lay the foundation, not of
any school of thought, but of human utility and power. I ask
them, then, to deal fairly by their own interests; to lay aside all
spirit of emulation, all prejudice in favour of this opinion or of
that, and to join forces for the common good. Freed by my help
and guidance from the errors and obstacles of the way, men must
come forward themselves and take their share
of the labours that remain.*

FRANCIS BACON, *Preface to The Great Instauration.* Sp. I, 132 (V, 21)

CHAPTER ONE

Bacon hopes to effect his reforms administratively

Though Bacon did not publish *The Great Instauration* till 1620, the years 1603-9 were decisive in the evolution of his thought. It was in this period, which brings him from the age of forty-two to forty-eight, that he first sought to give extended literary expression to his philosophical views. During these years he began nine works, of which he finished only four and published only two.[1] Pressure of public business goes some way to explain the unfinished works. Having been neglected by Elizabeth he begins to be noticed by James. But the deeper explanation lies, as we shall see, in the rapid evolution of his thought. He was still feeling his way. The decision, however, not to publish finished works has a different cause. Bacon intended his philosophy to bear fruit in practice and feared to court failure by premature disclosure. The time was not yet ripe. 'Till about the year 1649', remarks that acute observer, Aubrey, 'twas held a strange presumption for a man to attempt an innovation in learning.' Consequently two of the finished works – *Thoughts and Conclusions* and *The Refutation of Philosophies* – were put into cold storage and left to his literary executors to publish. The two which he did publish – *The Advancement of Learning* and *The Wisdom of the Ancients* – were designed to prepare the public mind for the later full disclosure of his views.

The purpose of this study is to follow the development of Bacon's thought through these seven years. This could not well be done without appending translations of the three most important of the posthumous works – *Temporis Partus Masculus*, *Cogitata et Visa* and *Redargutio Philosophiarum* – modern versions of which are easier to find in Italian than in English.[2] It is true that

---

1. List of Bacon's writings 1603-9. The first five are unfinished.

1603 Temporis Partus Masculus	1604 Cogitationes de Natura Rerum
1603 De Interpretatione Naturae Procemium	1604 Cogitationes de Scientia Humana
1603 Valerius Terminus of the Interpreta- tion of Nature, with Annotations of Hermes Stella	1605 The Advancement of Learning
	1607 Cogitata et Visa
	1608 Redargutio Philosophiarum
	1609 De Sapientia Veterum

2. *Temporis Partus Masculus* and *Redargutio Philosophiarum* in *La Nuova Atlantide e Altri Scritti* by Paolo Rossi, Milan, 1954; *Cogitata et Visa* in *Per il progresso della scienza* by Manlio Rossi, Milan, 1934.

Spedding, anxious to economise space, offered no English version of these three funda-

the substance of these writings was later more or less completely absorbed into the body of *The Great Instauration*. But this does not rob them of their importance. Spedding, when editing the collected works, spoke of them as 'among the most interesting of the whole collection' because 'in them we may trace more than can be traced elsewhere of what may be called the *personal* history of his great philosophical scheme.'[1] Biographically they are indispensable.

The germ of Bacon's philosophy obsessed his mind from boyhood. This is well known. What is not always remembered, or perhaps realised, is that at first he thought of introducing his reform administratively. Administrative action was a natural line, considering his family position, for his ambition to take. His father Sir Nicholas, and his uncle Lord Burleigh were long the twin pillars of the realm. He was his father's favourite son, and though he was but eighteen when his father died, he had already begun to be seasoned in affairs by his residence with the English ambassador at the French court. After his father's death his uncle was still supreme among Elizabeth's councillors. Francis distinguished himself at his legal studies, entered Parliament at twenty-four and at once made his mark.

It was at this time, as we learn from a remark of his own, that he first committed his philosophical ideas to writing. The essay, which bore the title of *Temporis Partus Maximus* (*The Greatest Birth of Time*) has not survived. It is doubtful if it was intended for publication. Rather he hoped by it to interest influential persons in his ideas and so achieve the means of putting them into execution. His father had been commissioned by Henry VIII to draw up a plan for a reform of education. The end in view was the training of a new type of lay administrator which had become necessary owing to the break with the mediaeval Church. Sir Nicholas's own draft does not survive. But we are reasonably certain of the kind of project he had in mind.[2] For though the plans were put in cold storage by Henry they were revived by Elizabeth, and eventually took shape, according to the ideas of Sir Nicholas Bacon, but at the hands of Sir Humphrey Gilbert, about 1570 as a

mental texts. Nothing of any value so far as these texts are concerned can be found in Peter Shaw's *Francis Bacon methodized and made English* (1733). In Basil Montagu's edition of the *Works* (1825–36) there is no version of *R.Ph.*, an incompetent and incomplete one of *T.P.M.*, but of *C. et V.* there is a scholarly rendering, not quite free from error, but worth the attention of anyone who has access to it.

1. Sp. III, 172.

2. Mark H. Curtis: *Oxford & Cambridge in Transition 1558–1642*, Clarendon Press, 1959, p. 67.

project for a University of London.[1] In this scheme languages were well provided for. Latin, Greek and Hebrew were to give the students the freedom of the old world; Spanish, French and Italian of the new. But the novelty lies elsewhere. Sir Humphrey bluntly states that he found 'the gentlemen of this realm for the most part good for nothing.' He proposes 'to make them good for somewhat' by giving them such a training in the practical arts as befitted an industrious and seafaring people at an epoch which economists now call the first industrial revolution.[2]

In this remarkable document, which reflected the ideas of Francis Bacon's father, we find it laid down that the professors on the science side were to engage in research. Their jobs were to depend on it. Every year they were to deliver to the Treasurer in plain language 'without equivocations or enigmatical phrases' a record of their experiments and results for their successors to build upon. It is relevant to remember the atmosphere of educational reform and policy-making in which Francis Bacon grew to maturity. It was almost certainly as a bid to become himself a policy-maker that he composed the lost treatise *Temporis Partus Maximus*. His first Parliament was that of 1584. It was notable for the number of university men who sat in it – 145 as compared with 67 in the Parliament of 1563. In a letter of 1625 to Fr Fulgentius, Bacon is quite precise in his statement that it was forty years earlier that he had written the book. That is shortly after he became a Member of Parliament. Bacon also plainly regards it as his first shot in a life-long campaign.[3]

Some seven years later, Bacon, now aged thirty-one, addressed a famous letter of appeal to his uncle Burleigh. It is still the chance to implement his reform administratively that he has in mind. In this letter he seeks what he calls a post 'of reasonable countenance', which would give him 'commandment of more wits than of my own, which is the thing I greatly affect.' If he can achieve this he hopes to reform educational policy by expelling scholasticism and alchemy. In their place he proposes 'to bring in industrious observations, grounded conclusions, and profitable inventions and discoveries.'[4] This defines the policy he pursued throughout the whole course of his life.

But, alas, there were good reasons why uncle Burleigh should not be

---

1. *Queene Elizabethes Achademy.* By Sir Humphrey Gilbert. Furnivall, Early English Text Society. Extra series No. viii, 1869.
2. John U. Nef: *Industry and Government in France & England 1540–1640.*
3. Sp. xiv, 533.   4. Sp. viii, 108–9.

impressed. He may not have cared much for scholasticism but his hopes had long been pinned on alchemy. Already in 1575 he had lost £100 in a scheme for converting iron into copper. Subsequently he kept in touch with Dr John Dee, who combined the practice of alchemy with mathematics, astrology and magic and it was in the year of the Armada that Dee sent home from Prague the news that Sir John Kelly had found the secret of transmuting base metals into gold. Burleigh, at his wits end to find money to finance the fleet, conjured Kelly not to keep God's gifts from his natural country; and in 1591, not many months before Bacon addressed to him the appeal quoted above, he pathetically besought Kelly 'to send her Majesty in some secret box some such portion of his powder as might be to her a sum reasonable to defray her charges for this summer for her navy which is now preparing for sea'.[1]

Elizabeth, herself, had other notions of how money might be raised and reasons of her own for not advancing Francis Bacon. She was pressing Parliament for an increased subsidy, and Bacon crossed her path. In a speech remarkable for its public spirit and its fatal brilliance of phrase, he said: 'The poor men's rent is such as they are not able to yield it . . . The gentlemen must sell their plate and the farmers their brass pots ere this will be paid. And as for us, we are here to search the wounds of the realm not to skin them over; wherefore we are not to persuade ourselves of their wealth more than it is.'[2] Those brass pots cooked Bacon's goose. The Queen never forgave him. Bacon, though he did not yet quite give up hopes of office, began to turn his thoughts in another direction. In his letter to Burleigh he had hinted that, if he had finally to forgo all hope of office, there would be nothing left for him but 'to become some sorry book-maker.'

And this he was soon to do, though not just yet. His friendship with Essex next presented him with hopes of high office. For it is certain that a common interest in the philosophy of works was a strong element, if not the very basis, of the attachment that sprang up between the two men.[3]

The concern of Essex for the progress of inventions showed itself in his connection with Sir Hugh Platt. In this key year of 1592, the ingenious Mr Platt (his knighthood came later – a gift from King James) exhibited to a select circle of Privy Councillors and leading citizens of London a series of mechanical inventions. Platt was of the opinion that 'the true end of all our private labours and studies ought to be the beginning of the public and

1. Conyers Read: *Lord Burghley and Queen Elizabeth*, Cape 1960, pp. 145–6 and 474ff.
2. Sp. VIII, 223.   3. Sp. VIII, 106.

common good of our country.' Two years later, when he published his *Jewel House of Art and Nature, containing divers rare and profitable inventions,* he dedicated it to Essex.[1] Bushell, the mining engineer, records that the gift of land by Essex to Bacon was in consideration of some ingenious meteorological contraption of Bacon's devising. The detail may be wrong, but the evidence as to the relation between the two men is good.

Essex now ran Bacon for two important posts under the Crown: first, for the Attorney-Generalship, then for the Solicitor-Generalship. He repeatedly risked, and incurred, the Queen's anger by the persistence and urgency of his pleas. Meanwhile the two men tried to disarm her hostility by a gentler and more circuitous approach. Essex devised entertainments for the Queen in 1592 and 1594 at which Bacon brought the claims of the new philosophy to her notice in the most ingenious and attractive guise. To the first of these 'devices' he contributed a *Discourse in Praise of Knowledge.* In it many of his basic propositions make their first public appearance. He condemns traditional learning because in all these hundreds of years it has failed 'to make us richer by one poor invention.' He attacks scholasticism and alchemy, 'whereof the one never faileth to multiply words and the other ever faileth to multiply gold.' He proclaims the necessity for what he calls 'a marriage between the mind of man and the nature of things.'

In the second 'device' he insinuates what practical steps he would take to implement the new philosophy if he had the power. He imagines a succession of councillors advising their prince on various topics and makes one of them say: 'I will wish unto your highness the exercise of the best and purest part of the mind, and the most innocent and meriting conquest, being the conquest of the works of nature ... To this purpose I will recommend unto your highness four principal works and monuments of yourself.' These turn out to be a research library; a botanical garden and zoo; a museum, not primarily of natural objects but of inventions ('whatsoever the hand of man by exquisite art or engine hath made rare in stuff, form, or motion'); and lastly a laboratory. Such was the programme of the would-be Minister for Science and Technology. But the Queen was not to be enticed. The joint campaign of Essex and Bacon met its final check; and the latter, bereft for the time being of all hope of office, began seriously to take up the trade of a sorry book-maker.

1. E. M. Tenison: *Elizabethan England,* Vol. IX, 1950, pp. 103, 104, 327–49.

CHAPTER TWO

First attempts at a literary presentation
of his plan

But this path also proved full of thorns. Much of what he wrote he decided not to publish. He was thirty-six when his first slim volume appeared. It contained a handful of *Essays* in English and a slightly larger handful of *Sacred Meditations* in Latin. To us now it is full of biographical interest; but the little volume could not have conveyed, was not intended to convey, any hint of his special philosophy to his readers. Eight years later came *The Advancement of Learning*, which does indeed begin to reveal the projected reform, but so cautiously that Bacon himself was later to call it 'a mixture of new and old' but not 'the new unmixed.'[1] Thirdly, in 1609, came *De Sapientia Veterum*, one of the deepest of his works. But, superficially at least, this attempt to derive wisdom from the fables of remote antiquity instead of from direct contact with nature, contradicts Bacon's fundamental position. We might justly be bewildered by these first-fruits of Bacon's pen did we not know that it was precisely in these years that he composed, along with other unpublished fragments, our three works, *The Masculine Birth of Time*, *Thoughts and Conclusions* and *The Refutation of Philosophies*. Hence the importance of our study. Bacon was involved in a problem of communication. He was publishing as much as he thought his public could take, but it is the unpublished works which preserve the full unmixed expression of his views and enable us to follow the development of his thought in the crucial years from 1603 to 1609, that is from the age of forty-two to forty-eight.

The first thing that strikes one on making the acquaintence of these works is the pent-up emotion that lies behind them. Bacon feels himself engaged on some great crusade affecting not simply the thought but the life of mankind. Professor Fulton Anderson, who has contributed much in recent years to the rehabilitation of our knowledge of Bacon, notes how, to the generations immediately succeeding his own, Bacon was the source of a host of exciting ideas, subsequently lost sight of.[2] For him Bacon is a man 'whose main passion in life was the good of mankind and the relief of the misery which belongs to his present estate'; a man, 'the crown of whose ambition was the direction

1. Sp. VII, 13.   2. *The Philosophy of Francis Bacon*. University of Chicago Press, 1948.

from a great place with magnificence and magnanimity of widespread and expensive scientific operations.' And he observes with amazement how he was reduced in the nineteenth century to a debatable figure in the history of inductive logic, 'a hesitant exponent of that empiricism which culminates in Hume.'

These are true words. Bacon's ambition was to make a new England, not a new logic. In his religious and moral outlook he was the child of that specifically English reformation, which centres round the names of Colet, Erasmus and More. Colet had imparted to Erasmus a conception of Christianity which put morality in the foreground and left dogma in the shade. Inspired by Colet, Erasmus became the most brilliant propagandist of the new evangel. But of all the group it was More in his *Utopia* who succeeded best in applying the new spirit to social problems. His revolt from the spectacle of English poverty led him, not only to advocate such revolutionary measures as leisure and education for manual workers, but to envisage, if not to recommend, the radical solution of an equal division of property.[1]

It is a mistake to look to Luther, Calvin or Ramus[2] for the moral or mental formation of Francis Bacon. The moralisation of religion; disgust at the contamination of the Gospel by the profane philosophy of Aristotle; the urge to find a radical solution for the problem of poverty; these fundamentals of Bacon's thought are of native English growth. But More's troubled speculation about an equal division of property had no appeal for him. He had something much more radical in mind. Not the subdivision of poverty, but the creation of plenty by the subduing of nature to the satisfaction of the necessities of mankind. This was the 'fructifying and begetting good' Bacon was set on achieving.

These remarks may serve to prepare the reader for *Temporis Partus Masculus* (*The Masculine Birth of Time*), which is the strangest, and, from the personal angle, one of the most illuminating of all his works. There has been discussion about the precise date of its composition. The title suggests a close relationship to the youthful *Temporis Partus Maximus* and this, together with the nature of the contents, has led Anderson to call it 'very early work.' But

---

1. F. Seebohm: *The Oxford Reformers of 1498*. London, 1867; A. Lagarde: *The Latin Church in the Middle Ages*. Edinburgh, 1915; W. E. Campbell: *Erasmus, Tyndale and More*, London, 1949; F. Caspari: *Humanism and the Social Order in Tudor England*, University of Chicago Press, 1954.

2. See *Henry Jackson, a Memoir* by R. St John Parry, C.U.P. 1926, p. 128, for a very choice specimen of very learned ignorance. Jackson thought Bacon 'no more than a populariser of Ramist principles in a country which did not know Ramus.'

Anderson can prove no more than that it must be earlier than 1603, when Bacon was forty-two, and it appears from the reference in it to the death of Peter Severinus, which occurred in 1602, that Bacon must have been forty-one or two when he composed it. It is impermissible, then, to explain its peculiarities, as Anderson does, by finding in it 'the unreflective ignorance and precipitate arrogance of an extremely precocious youth'. The peculiarity of the writing is due to the fact that Bacon is undertaking a novel task. He had counted on introducing his reform administratively and now finds himself under the necessity of winning support for it by a written argument which will convince the learned world. He has not yet taken the measure of the task. He thinks to carry the day by strength of feeling and is too impatient to develop his thoughts. The two later writings will correct these faults. We are in the workshop of one of the great minds of one of the great ages of the world.

The sub-title shows that Bacon had already found the formula which was to do duty about twenty years later for his supreme masterpiece. It runs *Instauratio Magna Imperii Humani in Universum* or *The Great Restoration of the Power of Man over the Universe*. This sub-title, of obviously biblical inspiration, is followed by the earliest version of a prayer repeated several times in Bacon's works:

'To God the Father, God the Word, God the Spirit, we pour out our humble and burning prayers, that mindful of the miseries of the human race and this our mortal pilgrimage in which we wear out evil days and few, they would send down upon us new streams from the fountains of their mercy for the relief of our distress: and this too we would ask, that our human interests may not stand in the way of the divine, nor from the unlocking of the paths of sense and the enkindling of a greater light in nature may any unbelief or darkness arise in our minds to shut out the knowledge of the divine mysteries; but rather that the intellect made clean and pure from all vain fancies, and subjecting itself in voluntary submission to the divine oracles, may render to faith the things that belong to faith.'

Elsewhere in Bacon's works this prayer bears the specific title of *The Student's Prayer*.[1]

The work proper, which is unfinished, consists of two chapters. It is in form a monologue addressed by an older man in authority to a younger man whom he calls 'son.' The first chapter is concerned with the transmission of knowledge and the point it makes is that the human mind is so beset by idols as to be incapable of accepting truth without some preparatory discipline.

1. Sp. VII, 259.

18

The young man will have therefore to accept a certain amount on trust. The speaker has something of the utmost moment to impart, but fears that it may be rejected before it is understood. This being in fact the fear which made Bacon suppress all the three writings with which we are here concerned, it is worth quoting his own statement of his difficulty. 'My intention is', the teacher is made to say, 'to impart to you, not the figments of my own brain, nor the shadows thrown by words, nor an adulterated form of religion, nor a few commonplace observations or notorious experiments tricked out to make a composition as fanciful as a stage-play. No: I am come in very truth leading to you Nature with all her children to bind her to your service and make her your slave. Does it seem to you then that I bear in my hands a subject of instruction which I can risk defiling by any fault in my handling of it, whether springing from pretence or incompetence? So may it go with me, my son; so may I succeed in my only earthly wish, namely to stretch the deplorably narrow limits of man's dominion over the universe to their promised bounds; as I shall hand on to you, with the most loyal faith, out of the profoundest care for the future of which I am capable, after prolonged examination both of the state of Nature and of the state of the human mind, by the most legitimate method, the instruction I have to convey.'

Packed into this brief paragraph are criticisms of Plato (figments of the brain), of Aristotle (shadows thrown by words), of Scholasticism (adulterated religion), of the various Renaissance philosophies (stage-plays), coupled with a burning profession of faith in the philosophy of works, the promise of a larger development of the doctrine of idols, and a suggestion of the necessity for a new scientific method. These insights, these purposes, these emotions, this sense of values, continue to characterise his work for the rest of his life. The brevity of the utterance should not be allowed to cloak its depth and originality. It is already a classic formulation of the mature convictions of the man.

The second and concluding chapter is a violent, even abusive, polemic against many of the greatest names, Greek, mediaeval and humanist, in the long history of thought. One after another Aristotle, Plato, Galen, Hippocrates; Thomas Aquinas, Duns Scotus; Paracelsus, Cornelius Agrippa, Peter Ramus, are summoned before the judgment seat, denounced and condemned. This might appear inexplicable did we not notice that the motive of the condemnation is rather moral than intellectual. The whole tradition of philosophy is rejected, and the fault that is found with it is not that its great men lacked ability, far from it, but that they lacked humility and charity.

CHAPTER THREE

Out with Aristotle and in with the Bible

This sweeping rejection of the whole tradition of philosophy – ancient, mediaeval and modern – has puzzling features which remained unexplained until the whole corpus of the Baconian philosophy was restored to its historical context. Many scholars working in various fields have contributed to the creation of the necessary understanding. But the harvest, so far as Bacon is concerned, has only recently been reaped. In a series of papers and books, covering the last five or six years, Professor Paolo Rossi of Milan has for the first time discussed adequately the Humanist and Renaissance literature which formed the background of Bacon's thought.[1]

The first point requiring explanation is the fierceness of the attack on Aristotle. From the Neoscholastic point of view this may easily appear incomprehensible. If one believes that 'Aristotle founded for all time the true philosophy'; that 'he definitively secured the attainment of reality by the human intellect'; and that consequently 'among philosophers he holds a position altogether apart'[2]; one will find it hard to forgive Bacon. Yet, for him, bent as he was on the attainment of the biblical promise to man of dominion over the creation, it was obvious that Aristotelianism had been ineffective for some two thousand years and must continue for ever to be so. For him all the current coin of Greek and Aristotelian philosophy – Earth, Air, Fire, Water; the Hot, the Cold, the Wet, the Dry; Matter and Void; Act and Potency – were merely labels attached to superficial knowledge at an early stage of its growth. No precision of definition or consistency of argument could alter this basic character. The urgent task was to fill all the terms with a new meaning by direct contact with things (cf. pp. 41, 83, 89).

Even the best descriptions of the steps by which the experimental method of modern Europe was reached may obscure the contribution of Bacon, unless his special aim is borne in mind. Professor Crombie's thesis, that 'the con-

---

1. *La Nuova Atlantide e Altri Scritti* (Milan, 1954); *Il Mito di Prometeo e gli Ideali della Nuova Scienza* (Rivista di Filosofia, Vol. XLVI, No. 2, 1955); *Francesco Bacone e la Tradizione Filosofica*, (Rendiconti Istituto Lombardo di Scienze e Lettere, Vol. LXXXVIII, 1955); *Sulla Valutazione delle Arti Meccaniche nei secoli xvi a xvii* (Rivista critica di Storia della Filosofia, Fasc. II, 1956); *Francesco Bacone: Dalla Magia alla Scienza* (Bari, 1957); *I filosofi e le macchine (1400-1700)*, (Milan, 1962).
2. Maritain, *An Introduction to Philosophy*, London, 1932, pp. 82-91.

ception of the logical structure of experimental science held by such prominent leaders as Galileo, Francis Bacon, Descartes, and Newton was precisely that created in the thirteenth and fourteenth centuries'[1], can mislead if it suggests that the science, say, of Roger Bacon in the thirteenth century was the same thing as that of Francis in the seventeenth. It is possible to miss the meaning of the later man's work by an exclusive attention to method. The spirit of his work was quite new. Roger, a product of the Hermetic school, looked upon scientific knowledge as a sort of revelation vouchsafed to a privileged class of *spiritual* men, incommunicable to the average run of *animal* men, and destined therefore to remain the preserve of an élite of initiates[2]. The life-work of Francis was to make the case for science as a publicly organised collaboration directed to the improvement of the conditions of life by the discovery of new arts.

But it is still necessary to ask why, in rejecting the Greeks, Bacon should with such determination have embraced the Bible. Why call his island utopia Bensalem (Son of Peace)? Why call the scientific institution, which was its vital centre, Solomon's House or The College of the Six Days' Works? Why make the narrative of the discovery of Bensalem a repository of biblical quotations (twenty-two from the Old Testament, ten from the New)? If these examples, being taken from a fiction, seem but the trappings of his thought, it must be remembered that the supreme masterpiece, *The Great Instauration*, is explicitly named with reference to the divine promise in *Genesis* of dominion over all creatures, and that the speculative type of philosophy derived from the Greeks is taken as the supreme example of the sin of pride, the occasion of the Fall, and therefore rightly cursed with barrenness. It is Bacon himself who insists that the heart of his meaning is biblical. He does not deny that the science of his day was derived from the Greeks. He merely protests that it is without benefit for the life of men and therefore not good enough for Christians. Listen to his own words:

'Your learning has come down from the Greeks. But what sort of nation was that? I want nothing abusive to be said; I shall neither repeat nor imitate what others have said. I content myself with the remark that that nation was always precipitate in genius and professorial by habit – two characteristics inimical to wisdom and truth. It would be wrong to pass by the words of

---

1. *Augustine to Galileo: The History of Science A.D. 400–1650*; *Grosseteste and the Origins of Experimental Science*, 1100–1750.

2. Rossi, pp. 92–4. R. Bacon, *Opus Tertium*, etc., ed. by J. S. Brewer, London 1859, pp. 42, 416, 543–4.

the Egyptian priest, spoken, as they were, to a distinguished Greek visitor and reported by a renowned Greek author. For the priest was a true prophet when he said, 'You Greeks are always children.' They were children not only in knowledge of history, but much more in the study of nature. What could be more childish than a philosophy prompt to chatter and argue, but incapable of procreation? A philosophy of futile disputations useless for works? Remember, then, as the prophet says (Isaiah 51, 1), the rock from which ye were hewn, and reflect that the nation whose authority you now follow was the Greek' (cf. p. 109).

The great quarrel between Hebrew and Greek is here given a new twist by Bacon but it is as old as Christianity itself. It begins with St Paul who observed, when he was in Athens, that 'the Athenians and the strangers in their midst had no time for anything but to tell or hear some new thing' (Acts 17, 21); and who urged the Colossians (Colossians 2, 8) 'to beware lest any man spoil you through philosophy and vain deceit.' From the beginning, in short, the Christian view was that the Greeks were a nation of talkers. But it was into a Greek-speaking world that Christianity was born. It was through the medium of Greek that Christianity made its first conquest of intellectual circles. It was under the influence of Greek logic and metaphysics that the creeds took formal shape. But this was not accomplished without the transformation of a predominantly moral and spiritual evangel into a metaphysical and intellectual creed. 'The change in the centre of gravity from conduct to belief', writes a nineteenth century authority, 'was coincident with the transference of Christianity from a Semitic to a Greek soil.'[1]

Latin Christianity was already formally united on the basis of Greek metaphysical creeds when, in the second half of the twelfth century, it received a fresh infusion of Aristotelian philosophy. On this foundation was erected in the thirteenth and fourteenth centuries the Scholastic system. It would be perverse to represent either this or any earlier or later incursion of Greek philosophy into Christian faith as wholly bad. But if we are to understand why the emergence of modern science, in so far as Francis Bacon was responsible for it, took the form of a revolt against Greek influences, we must try to see the situation through seventeenth century English eyes. Here the great Anglican historian of ecclesiastical literature, Dr William Cave, can help us.[2]

According to Cave, then 'in the first centuries of the Church the Apostles

1. Edwin Hatch, *The Influence of Greek Ideas on Christianity*. Hibbert Lectures, 1888.
2. *Scriptorum Ecclesiasticorum Historia Literaria*, 1688. I have used the Geneva ed. of 1705.

and their successors handed on the pure and simple doctrine they had received from Christ in a clear and easy style adapted to the understanding of the common man.' Then, over the centuries, a gradual transition took place, first in Greek and then in Latin Christianity, from simple preaching to dialectical instruction. This process had already established itself with Abelard (1079–1142) and Peter Lombard (1100–60). 'Theology now became a form of disputation adapted to deal with perpetually recurring doubts; it was restricted to the purpose of philosophical instruction; it was split up into an infinity of small questions discussed for and against; it was carried, with an excess of zeal, into the most trifling distinctions.' 'As was to be expected, theologians now drew apart into opposing sects: Nominalists and Realists, Thomists and Scotists, *Sententiarii* and *Quodlibetarii*, perpetually engaged in mutual broil. The simpler and purer doctrine of the ancients was abandoned and Scholasticism assumed a monopoly of teaching in Christian schools. Thus the philosophy of Aristotle, which had been brought in as a support, extended its empire over theology itself, with the result that for some centuries Aristotle virtually usurped the seat of St Paul.'

The triumph of Aristotle over St Paul was not only intellectually but morally disastrous. The spirit of persecution culminating in the Inquisition was the outcome of attempting to base religious unity on metaphysical dogmas. 'When those charged with the task realised that the heretics could not be brought back to the bosom of the Church by force of words they sent against them warriors bearing the sign of the cross and, as a further step in keeping with their pious purpose, set up the Office of what they called the Holy Inquisition, though in fact it was the heavy disgrace of the Christian religion, a thing fetched from Hell to be the executioner of consciences and the enactor of such tyrannies as the cruel ingenuity of the Sicilian tyrants could not match.'[1] Bacon was no bigot. Of his many good friends the closest was Toby Matthew, a convert to Romanism. But Cave's opinions were his opinions, and the name of Aristotle stands for him as that of a corrupter of religion and the diverter of human knowledge from fruitful works to mischievous disputations.

Now the chief agent of the overthrow of Scholasticism in English minds was the Bible. In the fourteenth century Wycliffe and the English Bible came in and Aristotle and Scholasticism began to go out. Eventually the two hundred arguments by which Duns Scotus convinced the Doctors in Paris of his latest theological innovation were to win him no more renown in Eng-

1. Cave, *Op. cit.*, pp. 615–6; Hatch, *Op. cit.*, pp. 310, 329, 349.

land than the derivation from his name of the word dunce. With the Bible came Hebrew studies. In 1540 a Chair of Hebrew was among the five Regius Professorships established by Henry VIII at Cambridge. Merchant Taylors' School, founded in 1561, taught Hebrew along with Latin and Greek from the first. The Reformation, in substituting an infallible Bible for an infallible Church, immensely stimulated Hebrew studies. Luther, Zwingli, Calvin were all Hebrew scholars. In England William Tyndale (1477–1536), unlike the Wycliffites, who based themselves on the Latin Vulgate, worked direct from the Hebrew. Bacon had for contemporaries and acquaintances, not only such a Jewish enthusiast as Sir John Finch, (his book *The World's Great Restoration or the Calling of the Jews* came out almost simultaneously with Bacon's *Great Instauration*) but also the great orientalist, Selden, who sat among the divines at the Westminster Assembly in 1643 saying: 'Perhaps in your little pocket-bibles with gilt leaves the translation may be thus, but the Greek or the Hebrew signifies thus or thus.' Even Bacon's aunts knew Hebrew, though his mother (and he) did not go beyond Latin and Greek. To sum up, in the fifty or sixty years after 1600 England passed from a mainly mediaeval to a mainly modern outlook on the world; this change coincided with the substitution for Aristotle of the Bible. The Authorised Version was the most influential book of the period.

'The English Reformation', says Trevelyan, 'which began as a parliamentary attack on Church fees, and proceeded as a royal raid on Abbey lands, was at last to find its religious basis in the popular knowledge of the Scriptures which had been the dream of Wycliffe.' 'The effect of the continual domestic study of the book upon the national character, imagination, and intelligence ... was greater than that of any literary movement in our annals, or any religious movement since the coming of Augustine.'[1]

Bacon was a conscientious and enthusiastic participant in this movement. 'That form of divinity,' he writes, 'which in my judgment is of all others most rich and precious, is positive divinity collected upon particular texts, not dilated into commonplaces, nor chasing after controversies, nor reduced into method of art ... For I am persuaded that if the choice and best of those observations upon texts of Scriptures which have been made dispersedly in sermons within this your Majesty's island of Britain by the space of these forty years and more had been set down in a continuance, it had been the best work in divinity which had been written since the Apostles' times.'[2] If Colet

---

1. *History of England*, pp. 310 and 367.
2. *Advancement of Learning* Bk. II. Sp. III, 487–8, slightly compressed.

CHAPTER FOUR

From the imitation of nature to the domination over nature

If Bacon had a philosophical precursor it was rather Bruno than Grosseteste or Roger Bacon. Bruno had been in England from 1583 to 1585, had had innumerable contacts with the livelier (and some less lively) minds, and towards the end of his stay published in London (although bearing the imprint either of Venice or Paris) a profusion of cosmological and ethical works.[1] In one of these, *Spaccio de la Bestia Trionfante* (*The Expulsion of the Triumphant Beast*) we find the expression of a revolutionary conception of science as power. 'The gods have given man intelligence and hands, and have made him in their image, endowing him with a capacity superior to other animals. This capacity consists not only in the power to work in accordance with nature and the usual course of things, but beyond that and outside her laws, to the end that by fashioning, or having the power to fashion, other natures, other courses, other orders by means of his intelligence, with that freedom without which his resemblance to the deity would not exist, he might in the end make himself god of the earth. That faculty, to be sure, when it is unemployed, will turn into something frustrate and vain, as useless as an eye which does not see or a hand which does not grasp. For which reason providence has decreed that man should be occupied in action by the hands and in contemplation by the intellect, but in such a way that he may not contemplate without action or work without contemplation. Thus, in the Golden Age, men, through idleness, were worth not much more than dumb beasts still are today, and were perhaps more stupid than many of them. But, when difficulties beset them or necessities reappeared, then through emulation of the actions of God and under the direction of spiritual impulses, they sharpened their wits, invented industries and discovered arts. And always, from day to day, by force of necessity, from the depths of the human mind rose new and wonderful inventions. By this means, separating themselves more and more from their animal natures by their busy and zealous employments, they climbed nearer to the divine being.'[2]

1. *Giordano Bruno*, by Dorothea Waley Singer, New York, 1950.
2. For the historical significance of this passage see R. Mondolfo, *En los Orígenes de la Filosofía de la Cultura*, Buenos Aires, 1960, chap. IV.

It is, of course, true that classical antiquity was not entirely devoid of the notion of the domination of man over the rest of creation:

> Sanctius his animal mentisque capacius altae
> deerat adhuc, et quod dominari in cetera posset.
> natus homo est.   OVID, *Metamorphoses* I, 75–8.[1]

So sang Ovid. And Cicero before him, in a long and splendid passage, had proclaimed: 'In short, by the use of our hands, we bring into being within the realm of Nature, a second nature for ourselves.' (*De Natura Deorum* II, 60.) Still there is in Bruno a new breath, a new vision, an enlarged horizon. His words are not a statement of a fact but a challenge; these words were published in England in a book dedicated to Sir Philip Sidney at the date, as near as can be determined, when Bacon wrote his lost *Temporis Partus Maximus*. Whether Bacon had met, or read, Bruno, both of which are probable considering what we know of the circles in which Bruno moved[2]; or whether mere coincidence is involved; certain it is that Bacon from about this date had become convinced that a new order of events was at hand, the specific quality of which would consist no longer in a mere *imitation* of nature but in her *domination* by man.

For Bacon the new vision was shaped in a pronouncedly biblical mould, nor is it difficult to see what advantages this had for his conception. There was scriptural authority for the new active science. Man was not a child of nature but a superior creature. At the same time, since God had made nature, the study of it was a religious duty, an act of worship, to be approached with humility and awe. Further, science, like religion, fell under the law of love. There were virtually only two commandments – to worship God and love your neighbour. To love your neighbour meant actively doing him good. Science which, in one aspect, was the worship of God, was also, by the application of knowledge to the relief of man's distress, the means of realising the love of one's neighbour. 'Science, like religion, must be judged by works.' So, on the one hand, Bacon cries out against those who 'look upon Art merely as a kind of corrective or supplement to Nature and do not allow Art the power to make radical changes and to shake Nature in her foundations'[3]; for 'in things artificial Nature takes orders from Man. Without Man such things would never have been made. By the agency of Man a new aspect

---

1. A holier creature than these and of loftier mind, capable of domination over the rest, was still to seek. Then Man was born.
2. Dorothea Singer, *Op. cit.*, chap. II.
3. *Sketch of the Intellectual World.* Sp. III, 730 (v. 506).

of things, a new universe, comes into view.'[1] On the other hand, the connection of this point of view with the Bible is explicitly asserted: 'Man by the Fall fell both from his state of innocence and from his dominion over the creation. Both of these losses can, however, even in this life, be in some measure recovered, the former by religion and faith, the latter by the arts and sciences. For the creation was not by the curse made altogether and forever rebellious to man. In virtue of that charter, *In the sweat of thy brow thou shalt eat bread*, but assuredly not by disputations nor by vain magical ceremonies, the creation is at length and in some measure being subdued to the supplying of man with bread, that is to say, with the satisfaction of his human needs.'[2]

Albert Schweitzer in his *Civilisation and Ethics* searches antiquity for evidence of an ethical will to effect a transformation of the world and finds it not. He has discriminating praise of Plato, but states justly that for him the true ethic is world-negation. He notes Aristotle's effort to avoid Plato's fate by turning from abstraction and seeking an empirical content of the Good, but finds that he, no more than Plato, rises above the limits of the city-state. Both distinguish between free and unfree (i.e. accept slavery) and have neither the idea of the Nation nor of Humanity as a whole. The Epicureans and the Stoics also are preachers of resignation. Even when we come to the rise of Christianity, he notes, the optimistic element in the world-view of Jesus was for long stifled by his teaching that the perfected world was to be the result of a catastrophic end to the natural order of things. The recovery of a world-affirming view was historically a slow process. It was not till the seventeenth century that it decisively prevailed. Schweitzer has but a qualified respect for Francis Bacon. He calls him 'an almost unphilosophic and moreover somewhat worm-eaten personality.' Nevertheless he acclaims him as 'the man who drafts the program of the modern world-view.' And true it is that Bacon exerted himself to banish the age-old pessimism of the philosophic tradition and rouse the human race from passive acceptance of ignorance, poverty and ill-health. He laboured to create both the knowledge and the will to attempt a transformation of the world. He was eager to insist that this overdue change was a 'birth of time.' But it was he who took the measure of the task, made it his life's work, and found the words that fired the imagination of mankind.

1. Sp. I, 395.   2. Sp. I, 365 (IV. 247–8).

CHAPTER FIVE

The ethical optimism of Bacon

It has seemed desirable to stress the ethical, optimistic, reforming zeal and determination of Francis Bacon because it is so generally neglected. Yet it expresses itself at every stage of his career. He confided to his private chaplain, secretary and friend, Dr Rawley, his early disgust with Aristotle. What is generally overlooked is that the reason for the disgust is not intellectual but moral. It rested solely on the fact that his writings were 'barren of the production of works for the benefit of the life of man.' 'In which mind,' adds Rawley, 'he continued to his dying day.' This was one of those adolescent moments of moral insight which determine the whole course of a life. Misunderstand this and you misunderstand the man. What Bacon confided to his friend Rawley he could only hint at to his uncle Burleigh. 'This', he writes to him of his plan of studies, 'whether it be curiosity, or vain-glory, or nature, or (if one take it favourably) *philanthropia*, is so fixed in my mind as it cannot be removed.' His *Sacrae Meditationes*, a neglected source for knowledge of his inmost mind, tells the same tale. Its main theme is charity, not in the modern sense of poor relief, but in the full sense of brotherly love as the fundamental Christian duty. The Second Meditation, on the miracles of Jesus, ends: 'He restoreth motion to the lame, light to the blind, speech to the dumb, health to the sick, cleanness to the lepers, sound mind to them that were possessed with devils, life to the dead. There was no miracle of judgment, but all of mercy, and all upon the human body.' The last sentence is characteristic. For Bacon charity meant meeting people's needs, not quarrelling with their opinions.[1]

Equally remarkable is the next meditation on *The Innocence of the Dove and the Wisdom of the Serpent*. Its problem is the special difficulty of those who aim, not at a private goodness, but at a public good. This was Bacon's case, and he observes that 'wicked men, who have not a wholesome thought in them, naturally assume that goodness springs from a certain simplicity of moral character and ignorance and inexperience of human affairs. Accordingly, unless they come to realise that every recess of their wicked hearts lies open to the understanding of him who is trying to move them, they treat him as a

1. For this and other references to *Sacred Meditations* see Sp. VII, 227ff.

fool.' Hence the need for the reformer to be seasoned in villainy. Which need not, however, soil him 'any more than light is soiled by falling on a privy.' In this self-imposed discipline of studying the workings of evil minds Bacon's preferred masters were Tacitus and Machiavelli.

The meditation on hypocrisy is also to the point. 'The ostentation of hypocrites is ever confined to the works of the first table of the law, which prescribes our duty to God. The reason is twofold, both because works of this class have a greater show of sanctity, and because they interfere less with their desires. The way to convict a hypocrite therefore is to send him from the works of sacrifice to the works of mercy. Whence the text: *Pure religion and undefiled before God and the Father is this, to visit the orphans and widows in their affliction;* and that other: *He that loveth not his brother whom he hath seen, how shall he love God whom he hath not seen?*'

Such was Bacon at the age of thirty-five. Six years later we have a direct fragment of autobiography and self-analysis.[1] Here he tells us that he believed he was born for the service of mankind. That after consideration of his own capacities and the needs of mankind he came to the fortunate conclusion that he was best fit to do what was most needed, namely to devote himself to the discovery of new arts, endowments, and commodities for the bettering of man's life; he felt this to be a nobler ambition than politics because what the statesman can do extends but over narrow spaces and lasts but short times, while the work of the inventor, though a thing of less pomp and show, is felt everywhere and lasts for ever. He allowed himself, however, to be deflected into politics both for family and patriotic reasons, and because he hoped that 'if I rose to any place of honour in the state, I should have a larger command of industry and ability to help me in my work.' Now, however, he finds his zeal mistaken for ambition; reflects that in waiting for the help and consent of others he is leaving undone the good he could do by himself alone; and accordingly, in pursuance of his old determination, is resolved to see what he can do by himself.

This is a description by Bacon himself of his state of mind at the time when he began the composition of *The Masculine Birth of Time*. The purpose of what he there calls his 'only earthly wish' was ethical, humanitarian, philanthropic. His new conception of science, to which we now turn, was incidental or instrumental to the accomplishment of this social end.

1. Sp. III, 518–20 (X, 84–7).

31

CHAPTER SIX

The upgrading of the manual arts

In the long passage from Bruno quoted in the fourth chapter two themes were intermingled. First there was the question of a real dominion by man over nature. In the second place, and intrinsically connected with it, was the dependence of this dominion on an alliance between intellectual and manual work, between head and hand. This second theme, also characteristic of the age, was exalted by Bacon into a fundamental principle of his philosophy. Later generations came unduly to narrow the scope of Bacon's projected reform by an exclusive emphasis on his method of induction. This was then taken to constitute his title to be the founder of experimental philosophy. But the generation immediately succeeding Bacon understood him better. Thus Tenison, Archbishop of Canterbury, when publishing in 1679 his valuable collection of *Baconiana*, says Bacon wanted to find out 'the several actions and passions of bodies' and how 'they may be made serviceable to human life.' 'Now this', he adds, 'was a work for a man of a thousand hands and as many eyes, and depended upon a distinct and comprehensive history of Nature.'

A thousand hands and a thousand eyes. Eyes, because this natural history was to be based upon extensive observation. Hands, because the more fundamental knowledge was to be derived from those mechanical operations by which man constrains nature. Implicit in this demand was a social as well as a philosophical revolution. The mechanical arts were to be rescued from their traditional contempt and restored to a central position in the history of civilisation. Here Bacon's proposals for educational reform went hand in hand with his political philosophy. He wished to wind up the feudal age in England and create a new England more on the pattern of the Dutch. He envisaged an England in which 'the wealth of the subject would be rather in many hands than few' and 'in hands where there is likest to be the greatest sparing and increase, and not in those hands wherein there useth to be the greatest expense and consumption'. Accordingly he directs men's eyes to 'our neighbours of the Low-Countries', whose 'wealth is dispersed in many hands and not ingrossed into few; and those hands not much of the nobility, but most and generally of inferior conditions'.[1]

1. Sp. VII, 60–1.

In the fifteenth and sixteenth centuries this revaluation of the role of the arts and crafts in the development of genuine scientific knowledge had many protagonists. Of these it will suffice to mention two who deeply influenced Francis Bacon. First is the French potter Bernard Palissy (1510–89). This extraordinary man, educated only in his craft, made striking advances in chemistry, geology, forestry and agriculture, and revealed in his writings the liveliest understanding of the social impact of techniques. When Bacon, still a youth, was resident at the French court, Palissy, already a famous man, was giving lectures and displaying his museum of natural objects to distinguished audiences. In his *Discours Admirables* (1580) Palissy writes: 'I can assure you, dear reader, that in a few hours, in the very first day, you will learn more natural philosophy from the objects displayed in this museum than you could in fifty years devoted to the study of the theories of the ancient philosophers.' This is Palissy's way of proclaiming the sovereign virtue of what Bacon was to call 'the commerce of the mind with things'; and it is now widely accepted that, either through attendance at his lectures or perusal of his book, Bacon was acquainted with the teaching of Palissy.[1]

Of even greater influence than Palissy, both in England and elsewhere, was the humanist Agricola, friend of Erasmus and Melancthon, exploiter of the Bohemian mines, and author of *De Re Metallica* (1546). His significance for Bacon lies not only in his account of the method of extraction of minerals and their uses, but in his sense of the influence of the mining industry on the history of civilisation. Important for Bacon also was his insistence on the need for clarity and precision of writing and copious and exact illustration. The Latin original was at once known in England. But the book was soon available also in a modern tongue under circumstances which suggest its reputation among the English in the middle of their first industrial revolution. Michael Angelo Florio, son of an Italian Jew who had become a Christian, fled to London, where he was befriended by Burleigh and appointed preacher to the Italian Protestant congregation. As an acceptable token of gratitude to his hosts he translated *De Re Metallica* into Italian and dedicated the volume to Queen Elizabeth in 1563.

The book was from the first an indispensable text-book, the perfect example of what Francis Bacon later called *experientia literata*, or dumb practice which has been to school and learned to express itself in writing. It put on record Agricola's experience of the Bohemian mines and made it available for application throughout the world. It enabled the Spaniards to

1. For the history of this view see Rossi, pp. 41–3.

exploit the inexhaustible mineral wealth of Bolivia. At Potosi the priests chained it to the altar so that the engineers, who perforce had recourse to it, might be reminded also of their religious duties. Of course the English used it too. Jean Bodin[1] says, in his praise of Agricola, that 'the Italians and Spaniards enlist the services of German and English mining engineers on account of their supernatural skill in locating metallic veins and opening them up.'

It is safe to say that Thomas Bushell did not get the Mendip and Cardiganshire mines into production without knowledge of Agricola. It was about 1608 or 1609 that he, then a boy of fifteen, entered the service of Francis Bacon, in which he remained so long as his master lived. All his life he acknowledged his debt to Bacon for the theory on which his very successful practice rested. A contemporary puff, in connection with his concession to work the Somerset mines, claims that the whole enterprise rested on 'the lord chancellor Bacon's philosophical theory in mineral discoveries, which (it is confessed) did light the first candle to these and all other mines of the like nature.'[2] It is difficult to know what this can mean except that Bacon, who had charged himself with the education of his protégé, introduced Bushell to the relevant parts of Agricola's book.

In any case, it is certain that Bacon knew the book. He alludes to it briefly, but with high praise, in De Augmentis.[3] Proof of an earlier appreciation of it may perhaps be found in Thoughts and Conclusions (chapter VIII). Animadverting on the stagnation of academic life, he exclaims: 'In the arts and sciences, as in mining for minerals, there ought everywhere to be the bustle of new works and further progress.' This image is likely to have sprung out of the pages of Agricola rather than actual experience of mines. However that may be, in this revaluation of the mechanical arts, in the collaboration which it implied between the scientist and the artisan, we find some part of the explanation of the rise of the modern world. Of this movement, if we may call Agricola the chief exponent in the sixteenth century, so certainly was Bacon in the seventeenth. But Bacon gave the theme a new dimension by considerations which find notable expression in the last two of the three writings which are our concern here.

1. *Methodus ad facilem historiarum cognitionem*, 1566.
2. See Blackbourne's edition of *Bacon's Collected Works*, London 1730, Vol. I, p. 150.
3. Sp. I, 572.

CHAPTER SEVEN

Mistaken tactics of The Masculine Birth of Time

We have been examining the character of Bacon's attack on Aristotle. Its fierce animus has two sources, the corruption of Christian doctrine by metaphysics and the corruption of science by a logic fertile in arguments but barren of useful arts. Bacon is not attempting a sober estimate of an historical figure. It is a living influence which he attacks.

The attack on Plato is also to be explained in terms of the contemporary situation. He, too, was an obstacle to science. 'He turned men's minds away from observation', Bacon explains, 'away from things, to which it is impossible to be too attentive and respectful.' But politically he was also a menace. Bacon allows him the 'merit of supplying table-talk for men of culture and experience of affairs, even indeed of adding grace and charm to everyday conversation.' This ironical concession springs from political hostility. The cultured classes in the England of Elizabeth were steeped in the Neoplatonism of Marsilio Ficino. This supplied the élite of wealth and birth with the ideal of an aristocratic type of state and with an aristocratic culture which made them, in the words of Sir Humphrey Gilbert, good for nothing. This aristocratic culture was incompatible with Bacon's philosophy of works which was but the reverse side of his programme of political reform. These reforms, affecting the court, the law, education, the Church and the Crown estates, were so far-reaching that, in the opinion of one of his biographers they might, if carried out, have prevented the revolution.[1] The struggle against Plato, like the struggle against Aristotle, has an immediate political relevance.[2]

In much the same way must we interpret the attacks on other great names. Galen and Hippocrates really stand for their modern followers who, by elevating them into unchallenged authorities, had halted medical progress. The valuable element in the attack is Bacon's optimistic conviction of the possibility of taking a great number of diseases off the list of those traditionally labelled incurable. The attack on sixteenth century writers hardly needs apology except for its violence. Cornelius Agrippa's *Occult Philosophy*,

1. Gardiner, in the *Dictionary of National Biography*; also Trevor-Roper, in *Past and Present*, No. 16, Nov. 1959, p. 64.
2. Rossi, *Op. cit.*, pp. 157–72; Caspari, *Op. cit.*, pp. 1–17.

in which were concentrated those Hermetic and Cabalistic influences Bacon justly condemned, was written before he was twenty-five, and the modern biographer can put it in its right perspective as the precocious performance of one who, all in all, was a gifted protagonist of Humanism and the Reformation. But it was the vanity of Agrippa to publish the book after he had come to disavow a large portion of its contents, and it was by this book he was known in the England of Bacon. So with Paracelsus. He had, in a degree far beyond Agrippa, the devotion to direct experimental study of nature, and by the modern historian is justly esteemed as the founder of iatrochemistry.[1] Nevertheless he had enough of the charlatan about him to supply justification for most of Bacon's harsh terms.

It would be beyond the purpose of this Introduction to discuss all Bacon's victims. But one, Peter Ramus, whom he calls 'a hide-out for ignorance, a pestilent book-worm, and a begetter of short-cuts to knowledge', must on no account be omitted. The abuse may at least make us wonder whether Henry Jackson was right in finding in Bacon 'no more than a populariser of Ramist principles in a country that did not know Ramus.' In fact the English knew Ramus very well and much appreciated him for adapting logic to a wider range of subjects than the theology of the Schools. The achievement of Ramus was to make logic apt for the handling of political and cultural topics; and the men of the Elizabethan Age, needing to transform themselves over-night into statesmen, courtiers, politicians and preachers, became enthusiastic Ramists. Even Bacon owed him a limited debt and in his *De Augmentis* accords him qualified praise.[2] But for Bacon in the period we are studying this outburst of Ramism was a superficial phenomenon masking the real problem. He drew a fundamental distinction between any form of logic, Aristotelian or Ramist, the purpose of which was to discover arguments, and that new logic of which he dreamed, the purpose of which was to discover arts. For Bacon there were two philosophies, two logics – one, already existent, valid in the sphere of ideas; the other, waiting to be born, valid in the sphere of natural reality. From this point of view there was, for Bacon, little to distinguish Ramus from Aristotle. Henry Jackson's dictum merely illustrates the deficiencies of Baconian scholarship in England even at the dawn of the twentieth century.[3]

So much it was necessary to say in justification of the judgments expressed by Bacon in *The Masculine Birth of Time*. The judgments, however harshly

1. Walter Pagel, *Paracelsus*. Basle and New York, 1958, esp. p. 349.
2. Sp. I, 668 (IV, 453).   3. Rossi, *Op. cit.*, pp. 348, 361, 369, 372, 446.

phrased, represent permanently held convictions. To understand them is to understand the essentials of his attitude. At the same time it may be admitted that the terms in which the judgments are phrased are a mistake. We must remember that we are here dealing with an unfinished as well as an unpublished writing. It seems to me evident from the turn of the monologue towards its conclusion that Bacon has begun to suspect that the style of abuse he has adopted is likely both to cause confusion and to give offence. His attempted defence, interesting as it is, probably did not satisfy even himself. The fact that he never resorted to it again is proof enough of this. As a piece of polemic the work is a failure. He recognised the fact and in what follows we shall see how he both mended his manners and deepened his thought.

CHAPTER EIGHT

Bacon rethinks his position. The sociology of knowledge

The Masculine Birth of Time is not the only unfinished work of Bacon's belonging to this transitional period of his thought. Elizabeth died in March 1603. Bacon had no reason to foresee as yet the series of advancements by the new King which would take him eventually to the Lord Chancellorship, and in July of 1603 we find him writing to Lord Cecil, from whom he had as little to hope as from his father, Lord Burleigh, 'My ambition now I shall only put upon my pen, whereby I shall be able to maintain memory and merit of the times succeeding.'[1] Bacon is still the author only of the *Essays* and the *Sacred Meditations*. There is, therefore, no reason to be surprised, considering both the inexperience of the writer and the magnitude of his theme, that he should have made several false starts. These we shall now consider. The dating of fragmentary writings given to the public in various collections after his death retains a margin of uncertainty. Furthermore, for the student of the development of Bacon's thought it is necessary to remember that a document correctly dated in a certain year, so far as the main body of it is concerned, might have received additions at a later date while it was still under the author's hand. With this caution the following dated sequence of writings will be found helpful.

In 1603 came *Temporis Partus Masculus*, discussed and translated in the present study; *De Interpretatione Naturae Procemium*, the autobiographical fragment already referred to on p. 31; and *Valerius Terminus*, an English work, which we must now briefly discuss.

Its title is mysterious. In full it runs thus: *Valerius Terminus of the Interpretation of Nature, with Annotations of Hermes Stella*. Of this title the only satisfactory explanation is that given by Anderson.[2] Bacon seeks to disguise his identity under a pseudonym. It must be remembered that his was a name which as yet carried no authority. The proposed pseudonym suggests the limit, perhaps we might say the 'true goal', to which the interpretation of nature could be pressed. But who is the Hermes Stella by whom the annotations, of which none are found, were to be supplied? Stella (star) is for

---

1. Sp. III, 256.   2. *Op. cit.*, pp. 16, 17.

Bacon a symbol of royalty. Hermes, or to give the full style only too familiar to an age deeply imbued with Hermetic literature, Hermes Trismegistus, thrice-great Hermes, is most naturally interpreted as a pseudonym for King James himself. Of him, Bacon was soon to say, in the *Introduction* to *The Advancement of Learning*, 'Your Majesty standeth invested of that triplicity which in great veneration was ascribed to the ancient Hermes: the power and fortune of a King, the knowledge and illumination of a Priest, and the learning and the universality of a Philosopher.' Bacon, it seems, was still dreaming, as under Elizabeth he had dreamt, and as under James he was to go on dreaming, of launching his programme under the aegis of the reigning monarch. But he failed with James as he had failed with Elizabeth.

The title, then, strongly suggests the perplexity in which Bacon was involved as to the best way of presenting his ideas to the public. But the contents show new features of the highest significance. These concern what were to be among the most important contributions made by Bacon to the progress of human knowledge. Of these we may consider three. First there is the full and clear statement, without polemics, of the distinction discussed at the end of the last chapter between two kinds of invention. 'Here I may be mistaken [misunderstood] by reason of some which have much in their pen the referring sciences to action and the use of man, which mean quite another matter than I do. For they mean a contriving of directions and precepts for readiness of practice ... But my intention contrariwise is to increase and multiply the revenues and possessions of man.'[1] Thus Bacon, in general terms, defines the difference between the logic of Ramus and his own.

The second and the third are concerned with two different kinds of obstacles to the attainment of the new knowledge for which Bacon is trying to clear the way. These obstacles may be classed as psychological and sociological. The psychological obstacles are the Idols of the Mind, already spoken of in *The Masculine Birth of Time*, but here given fuller development. Thus in his sixteenth chapter he proposes to treat of 'the inherent and profound errors and superstitions in the nature of the mind, and of the four sorts of Idols or false appearances that offer themselves to the understanding in the inquisition of knowledge. That is to say, the Idols of the Tribe, the Idols of the Palace, the Idols of the Cave, and the Idols of the Theatre.' There is a difficulty about the Idols of the Palace, which are not mentioned except in this work and do not admit of a ready explanation. Elsewhere we read, instead, of the Idols of the Forum or of the Market-place; and I should think

1. Sp. III, 235.

it certain that Palace here is no more than a scribe's mistake for Place. Unless the sketch for this chapter is a late addition we therefore find Bacon already in 1603 in possession of his four types of mental obstacles to the acquisition of a true knowledge of Nature, viz: (1) those arising from our human nature (Idols of the Tribe), (2) those arising from the nature of language (Idols of the Market-place), (3) those arising from the circumstances and education of the individual (Idols of the Cave), (4) those arising from the errors of learned men (Idols of the Theatre).

To set human knowledge thus in a new light, to provide a powerful technique for analysing its distortions, is the revolutionary achievement of the psychological doctrine of Idols. Connected with this and no less remarkable is Bacon's doctrine of the sociological distortion of truth. This is the subject of the twenty-sixth and last chapter of *Valerius Terminus*. Here he considers, '*The impediments which have been in the nature of society and the policies of state. That there is no composition of estate or society, nor order or quality of persons, which have not some point of contrariety towards true knowledge.*' No later work of Bacon will fail to bear the imprint of the thought expressed in the sentences here italicised. It is the source of the doctrine of Signs developed in the *Refutation* and perfected in the *Novum Organum*. Idols are a disease of the individual mind. Signs reveal the short-comings of an epoch. They indicate that the systems of philosophy in use are in a bad condition and thus prepare the way for a more gentle and easy extirpation of Idols from the understanding.[1]

To the next year, 1604, belong two more unfinished works, *Cogitationes de Natura Rerum* (*Thoughts on the Nature of Things*) and *Cogitationes de Scientia Humana* (*Thoughts on Human Knowledge*). The first of these writings contains in its third chapter, *On the Negligence of the Ancients in the Enquiry concerning Motion and the Moving Principles of Things*, a singularly clear statement of what Bacon considered to be the difference between the contemplative science of the ancients (together with their modern imitators) and the operative science at which he himself aimed. It is worth quoting, at least in part, since, without vituperation or even the bare mention of any names, it gives a coolly reasoned statement of the grounds for his passionate rejection of the ancient view. 'One whose object is to achieve an active natural philosophy must concern himself principally with the investigation of motion. To investigate, or exercise one's imagination, about the inactive principles of things is fit only for one whose purpose is to provide matter for talk and

1. Sp. I, 180 (IV, 71).

disputation. By inactive principles I mean those which tell us what thing consist of but not by what force or in what manner they come together A man might have by him a true description of the materials used for making sugar, glass, and cloth without the knowledge of the processes of making them. Yet speculation has been principally concerned with the investigation of these dead principles, as if a man should make it his business to anatomise the corpse of nature without enquiring into her living faculties and powers. So in the fashionable philosophies we read of privation, form, the attraction of like to like, the random agitation of atoms in the void, strife and friendship, interaction between heaven and earth, the grouping of the elements by symbolising qualities, the influence of celestial bodies, sympathies and antipathies, specific hidden virtues and properties, fate, fortune, necessity. *But such generalities as these are mere phantoms that float on the surface of things. I need hardly ask whether they can enrich mankind or increase the number of his possessions. They merely inflate the imagination and are of no effect towards the accomplishment of works.'*[1]

From the second of the fragmentary works that belong to this year, that called *Thoughts on Human Knowledge*, I choose to illustrate one topic which continued throughout Bacon's life to grow in importance. That is his plan for a Natural History of a new type. Since this plan forms part of a long and brilliantly managed argument not translated by Spedding and, so far as I am aware, not available elsewhere in English, I propose to translate a large part of the article.

'If we are to have a purer Natural Philosophy, its foundations must be solidly based in Natural History, and a Natural History which is both copious and accurate. A philosophy derived from any other source is as unstable as water and as gusty as wind, and has no bearing on the active side of philosophy and human needs. To make the point still more clear, a Natural History resting on insufficient research and insufficient testing begets two faults and, as it were, two diseases or corruptions of theory. The first results in sophistry, the second in poetry. Take first a man, who, on the basis of commonplace observations, constructs a specious theoretical system and relies for the rest exclusively on his discursive and argumentative ingenuity. His discoveries may be so fortunate as to win a great reputation, but he himself is nothing more than a survivor of the old sophistic school. Take again a man who conducts a thorough and carefully controlled investigation of a portion of the field. If he is puffed up by this and allows his imagina-

1. Sp. III, 19–20 (V, 424).

41

tion free play he may be led to interpret the whole of nature after the pattern of the little bit he knows. His philosophy then passes into the realms of fancy or dreaming and consigns him to the category of the poet.

'We should therefore recognise the depth and penetration of that saying of Heraclitus, who protested against those who sought their philosophy in their own private worlds instead of in the great public world. Such men have only a touch of Natural History, but yet indulge themselves in endless speculation with only a feeble capacity to distinguish between the two.'[1]

'Of this weakness the most astonishing example is Aristotle. He was a great man, financed by a great king, familiar with natural and civil history, the author of a notably accurate *History of Animals*, who moreover, as is clear from his *Problems* and *Parva Naturalia*, had devoted much thought to all sorts of researches, and who even allowed the senses their proper role. Nevertheless his Natural Philosophy is divorced from things; he notoriously deserted experience; and, however men may seek to hedge and quibble, produced as the result of his mighty exertions something much closer to Logic than to Physics or Metaphysics.

'Thus it came about that Aristotle with his impetuous and overbearing wit was a sufficient authority to himself, despised his predecessors, compelled experience to lend a servile support to his own views and led her about like his captive slave, and, in view of the commotion he had made, donned Pluto's helmet, or, in other words, walked about concealed in a cloud of artificial obscurity. Finally he shielded himself behind his Logic, alleging with more licence than truth that he had invented it himself, forced facts to dance attendance on his words, and by the self-seeking and cunning use to which he turned it corrupted the great variety of his learning and knowledge.

'Now I myself have not the ability to fashion a statue of Philosophy and set it up; but I might aspire to prepare a base for such a statue and I recommend to men as the first essential the recognition of the usefulness and dignity of Natural History.' Bacon then discusses what men have hitherto understood by Natural History and adds: 'My idea, however, is very different. The kind of Natural History I am seeking is one from which natural causation can be understood, on which Philosophy can be based, which is faithful to sense-evidence and proved by works.' The most important and the most neglected element in this new Natural History will be 'mechanical

1. Here follows the famous sentences on the degenerate learning of the Schoolmen, which, since they are repeated in the *Advancement*, Bk I, Sp. III, 285, and are familiar, I omit.

history or the history of the arts, to which no man has ever applied himself, on which no man has ever expended the unbroken toil which is its due.'[1]

The writings of these two years reveal an author at the height of his genius. But though he is teeming with new ideas he is still uncertain how to put them forward. He tries Latin, he tries English. He wonders if a dramatic monologue will not be more effective than a straight exposition. At one moment he is violently polemical, at the next urbane. He wonders whether it would not be best to suppress his own name and write under a pseudonym. At last, in 1605, the problem of presentation finds a provisional solution. He had published nothing since the *Essays* and *Sacred Meditations*, unless we are to take into account a defence of his conduct vis-à-vis Essex and a pamphlet concerning *The Better Pacification and Edification of the Church of England*. Now comes out a big book, *The Advancement of Learning* (1605), which, in spite of signs of haste in construction and writing, holds a great place in European literature. Here Bacon shelves his main problem by soft-pedalling his novel ideas for the reform of natural philosophy and exploits the vast resources of his knowledge and reflection to speak his mind on the general topic of the present state and future prospects of learning.[2]

This buoyant and confident piece of writing owes its modernity not to its advocacy of science in the narrow sense of the term. Bacon is not here producing, would not have been capable of producing, a generalised expression of the mentality of the creators of modern science. He is not the spokesman of Vesalius, Copernicus, Galileo, Gilbert or Harvey. What he could do was something different. His dominant interest was in the conditions of human life. He had a vivid appreciation of the role hitherto played in history by technology, and a vivid anticipation of the much greater effect that could be wrought on human life if technology could be made scientific. As the necessary preliminary to this change he wanted technology to be made 'literate.' Leibniz, who got the idea from Bacon, has given it forceful expression: 'The unwritten knowledge dispersed among men of various trades far exceeds in quantity and importance all that has yet found its way into books.' The accumulated and sifted information to be drawn

1. Sp. III, 187–92.
2. In Bk. II (Sp. III, 332–3) there is indeed a sort of manifesto declaring Bacon's conviction of the unique importance of a study of the mechanical arts for the foundation of a true philosophy of nature. But this is left without a relevant context. It is only in the expanded Latin version of *The Advancement – De Augmentis* II, 2 (Sp. IV, 297–8) and V, 2 (Sp. IV, 447–421) – that the context is supplied. But this was after 'the new unmixed' had already been given to the world in *The Great Instauration*.

from the experience of the arts and crafts would provide the basis for the next step, namely controlled experimentation leading to higher axioms disclosing the deep and hidden workings of nature. The programme is wrongly described as utilitarian, since for Bacon the knowledge of nature was part of the worship of God, and the most effective way of fulfilling the law of charity. But the obstacles to this attainment lay deep in the nature of the human mind and could not profitably be discussed without reference to cultural history. The very nature of language involved each new generation in the errors of the old by the process of learning to speak. The technological, political, social and religious history of the race, entangled scientific advance with every other aspect of human life. While Bacon could therefore later say, in criticism of *The Advancement of Learning*, that in it he had given 'a mixture of the new and old', and not yet 'the new unmixed', yet his caution was necessary and the book, even within its self-appointed limits, powerfully forwarded his purpose. In the *Advancement* he defines what he understands by the history of science and notes it as wanting. 'A just story of learning, containing the antiquities and originals of knowledges, and their sects; their inventions, their traditions; their diverse administrations and managings; their flourishings, their oppositions, decays, depressions, oblivions, removes; with the causes and occasions of them, and all other events concerning learning throughout the ages of the world; I may truly affirm to be wanting. The use and end of which work I do not so much design for curiosity, or satisfaction of those that are lovers of learning; but chiefly for a more serious and grave purpose, which is this in few words, that it will make learned men wise in the use and administration of learning.'[1]

1. Sp. III, 330.

CHAPTER NINE

Thoughts and Conclusions, The Refutation of Philosophies

In default of that 'just story of learning' which would serve the 'serious
and grave purpose' of making 'learned men wise in the use and administration of learning', Bacon sets out to do his best with the new historical insights at which he had arrived. He switches his attack from individuals and
concerns himself with the psycho-social conditions hindering the emergence
of a genuine natural philosophy. Errors are exposed in the course of discov-
ering their cause. Plato and Aristotle, Cicero and Seneca, are no longer
individuals to be chastised, but representatives of determinate cultural
epochs. The civilisations of Greece and Rome are each shown to have had
features inimical to the pursuit of natural philosophy, and so with the Early
Church. A Schoolman in his cloister could not be in touch with the busy
changing world. Neither the Humanist, bent on reviving Classical antiquity,
nor the Reformer, bent on reviving Christian antiquity, could respond
adequately to the discovery of new lands or new inventions: 'Delicate
learning', not active science, was to be expected of them. The feudal land-
owner would look out on the world with different eyes from the merchant
or the manufacturer. So Bacon takes stock of his world, its institutions and
traditions, national temper, public policies, sectional interests, and seeks again
the best means of presenting his plan to those who, for one reason or another,
might be expected to misunderstand and condemn.

The first result is *Thoughts and Conclusions*, nineteen separate chapters
directed each to expounding an aspect of the plan and meeting the antici-
pated objections. Each chapter presents a train of thought followed by a
conclusion. This essential structure of the little work is obscured by Anderson, who mistranslates the title *Thoughts and Impressions*. What it offers is not
a series of musings but of cogent arguments brought to a precise point. The
whole work is written in the third-person, like Julius Caesar's *Commentaries*,
and creates a similar expression of a proud self-effacement. *The Refutation
of Philosophies* repeats much the same matter in a different style. The argument is now presented, in the manner of Plato's *Laws*, as a discourse by an
Unknown Stranger to a Parisian audience of men of various nationalities

45

experienced in affairs of Church and State. The character of the speaker is carefully drawn, rather like Bacon pretending to be a Frenchman, a little more man-of-the-world than his usual self.

Both writings, in style and content, show Bacon at the height of his genius. Their substance was later worked up afresh in aphoristic style to form the First Book of *Novum Organum*, but this hardly detracts from their interest. What Bacon thought worth presenting in two different styles with different illustrative matter is worth our attention. The two statements support and illustrate one another. Unlike Plato, who thought rhetoric a voluptuary art ministering only to pleasure and on the same level as that of the cook, Bacon thought the function of rhetoric was to minister in one way or another to reason. Here we can study his theory in application as he seeks either to convince the reason, rouse the will, or serve the memory, all three processes being the preliminary to rational action. Least of all should we suppose that Bacon's failure to publish these writings meant that he condemned them. He only feared they might not at that juncture achieve their purpose. To assist his judgment on this point he submitted them to chosen friends, how many we do not know. It seems certain that his most congenial friend, Toby Matthew, approved. We do not know whether Lancelot Andrewes (then reluctantly busy composing his *Tortura Torti* to confute Cardinal Bellarmine) ever found time to express an opinion. Sir Thomas Bodley, in a long letter which is innocent of any true understanding of what Bacon was at, made it plain that neither he himself nor any sober body of academic opinion would stand for Bacon's plan.[1] Bacon seems to have taken this as decisive for the immediate fate of his two choice writings. He was without literary ambition in any personal sense. There was a work he wanted done. These writings would not further it just then. He left them to his literary executors for publication after his death.

Furthermore, the possibility of carrying out his project actively now again presented itself, and in two ways. In the first place, his political prospects revived. Two days before the coronation of James, Bacon was knighted. He was but one of a batch of three hundred; still it was a mark of favour. Then, in 1607, the lesser of the two offices Essex had tried to secure for him from Elizabeth was granted him by James. He became Solicitor-General. Next year he had another piece of luck. The reversion to the Clerkship of the Star Chamber, which he had long held, fell in and brought with it a

1. Sp. x, 366. The letter, dated Fulham, 19 Feb. 1607, is to be found in *Trecentale Bodleianum*, Oxford, Clarendon Press, 1913.

substantial increase of fortune. He now had about £5,000 a year, and if all he had wanted was to set up a private laboratory and start experimenting himself, this was the chance. But, of course, that was not what he wanted. He had no particular line of research like Gilbert or Harvey; he had only a consuming belief that if a great number of investigations could be put in hand simultaneously they would illuminate one another and provide that accumulation of material on which a genuine philosophy of nature might be based. One way to his goal, therefore, was to cultivate the King's favour and hope for further advancement.

But there was also another way. His private diary for 1608[1] reveals that Bacon had thought of a fresh plan by which he might get command of the necessary wits and pens. His idea was to get himself made head of some school or college. Westminster, Eton, Winchester; Trinity or St John's in Cambridge; Magdalen in Oxford, are the places he thinks of. It is entertaining to speculate what the future of education in England might have been if he had secured control of one of these institutions and installed the vaults, furnaces and laboratories which he says in his diary he would need. He devotes much thought to the idea. He thinks of approaching Sir Thomas Russell (who, with government sanction, was engaged at the time in experiments for separating silver from lead ore) for 'a collection of phenomena concerning surgery, distillations, mineral trials.' He has a plan 'to set on work' My Lord of Northumberland; Sir Walter Raleigh, who was Warden of the Stannaries; and the mathematician Harriot, all three of them, Bacon notes, 'themselves being inclined to experiment.' He pricks off the names of three eminent physicians as likely to understand and help – Dr Poe, Dr John Hammond, Sir William Paddy. He thinks it worth trying whether Richard Bancroft, Archbishop of Canterbury, 'being single, and glorious, and believing in the sense', might not be drawn in. Then there is his old friend, Bishop Lancelot Andrewes. It has been thought cynical that Bacon includes him among possible sources of help on the grounds of his being 'single, rich, sickly, a professor to some experiments.' But Bacon himself left directions (though, as it turned out, not adequate provision) in his own will to further scientific research. What is there cynical in hoping his rich friend would do the same? The money would have been as well spent as the £3,000 it cost the wealthy bishop to entertain King James for a few days.

Of these two prospects it was the first that was realised. Bacon did not succeed in turning some grammar school or university college into a scienti-

1. Sp. XI, 63-73.

fic and technological institute. He did become Attorney-General in 1613, Lord Keeper in 1617, Lord Chancellor in 1618, and it was from that high station that two years later, when he was on the verge of sixty, he, for the first time, in *The Great Instauration*, presented his programme to the world. Meanwhile, when he suppressed *Thoughts and Conclusions* and *The Refutation of Philosophies*, he sought the same kind of compromise as before. His *De Sapientia Veterum* (*Wisdom of the Ancients*), like the *Advancement*, was designed to be a mixture of old and new, a softening-up operation, in anticipation of the time when he could issue the new unmixed. Published in 1609 this brilliant and popular work[1] rises as naturally out of the unpublished writings of 1607 and 1608 as the *Advancement* did out of the unpublished writings of 1603 and 1604. Though it is in a sense a compromise, its true significance is great. It was ill-placed by Spedding not among the philosophical but among the literary works. To Anderson and, after him, to Rossi, we owe the full understanding of its place in the Baconian philosophy of works.

During the composition of *Thoughts and Conclusions* and *The Refutation of Philosophies*, Bacon remained faithful to his old protestation that 'science is to be sought from the light of nature, not from the darkness of antiquity.' But, as he deepened his historical studies and his historical insight, he became more and more impressed with the achievement of the Presocratic philosophers. He sensed in their fragments a more direct contact with nature than in later Greek schools and, in his enthusiasm, made a pioneer study of their scattered remains which was to be of importance for the scholarship of the nineteenth century. He developed a preference for the materialism of Democritus over the idealism of Plato; and his sense of the superiority of the natural philosophy of Empedocles and Democritus over the logic and metaphysics of Aristotle and Plato became the chief example, if not the very foundation, of his view that the river of time bears down to us on its surface the slighter and emptier relics of the past and drowns the more solid achievements in its depths.

The formation of this private conviction in Bacon's mind coincided with an intense curiosity of the age about the true meaning and interpretation of fables and myths. This, which was by no means a trivial subject of enquiry, had given rise in Italy to a series of notable books. Boccaccio's fourteenth century *Genealogy of the Gods* was the precursor in sixteenth century Italy of several studies which had prompt and powerful repercussions in England.

1. It came out in Latin in London in 1609 and 1617, in English in two separate editions in 1619, and in French at Paris in the same year.

Of these Italian books the most relevant to our enquiry is Natale Conti's *Mythology* (1515). In it Bacon read these words: 'In ancient times all philosophical learning was cloaked in fables. Indeed, not so many years before the times of Aristotle and Plato and the rest of the philosophers, all philosophical doctrines were handed on, not openly but obscurely, wrapped up, as it were, in a veil.'[1] What Bacon made of this may be read in his own words: 'The most ancient times (except what is preserved of them in the Scriptures) are buried in oblivion and silence: to that silence succeeded the fables of the poets: to those fables the written records that have come down to us. Thus between the hidden depths of antiquity and the days of tradition and evidence that followed there is drawn a veil, as it were, of fables, which come in and occupy the middle region that separates what has perished from what survives ... It may be that my reverence for the primitive times carries me too far, but the truth is that in some of these fables, as well in the very frame and texture of the story as in the propriety of the names by which the persons that figure in it are distinguished, I find a conformity and connexion with the thing signified, so close and evident, that one cannot help believing such a signification to have been designed and meditated from the first, and purposely shadowed out.'[2]

With this much justification, warning us neither to press his interpretation too hard nor altogether to disbelieve it, Bacon proceeds to draw, out of thirty-one fables of classical antiquity, a rounded exposition of his views on the nature of scientific knowledge and its bearing on politics, religion and morals. Pan becomes Nature, Orpheus philosophy, Uranus the origin of things, Proteus matter, Cupid the atom, Prometheus the human condition, Daedalus the mechanic. By this allegorical method of interpretation the gravest of problems touching the use and administration of knowledge are disarmingly presented as the reasonable significance of these venerable old fables. It is an exercise in a fashionable form of literature in which serious speculations about the wisdom of antiquity are blended with the author's most cherished convictions of what mankind should now do. The seventeenth century easily took Bacon's meaning. Archbishop Tenison calls it a book 'in which the sages of former times are rendered more wise than it may be they were by so dexterous an interpreter of their fables.' This is to recognise that the doubtfulness of the attributions to antiquity is quite compatible

---

1. See Rossi, *Op. cit.*, chap. III, and the *Mythologia* of N. Conti, opening sentences of Bk x. But Bacon owes nothing except his point of departure to Conti.

2. *Preface* to *The Wisdom of the Ancients.* Sp. VI, 695–6.

CHAPTER TEN

Magic, Alchemy and Modern Science

One other puzzle in Baconian scholarship has defied full elucidation till our day, namely, Bacon's ambivalent attitude to magic and alchemy. For the most part he denounces them roundly; he is also plainly heavily in their debt. Rossi's achievement here is both to have defined the debt and justified the denunciation.

First for the debt. In *Sylva Silvarum*, that hasty compilation of already existing natural knowledge on which Bacon worked so feverishly in the shadow of approaching age, he guilelessly takes from magico-alchemical sources many of their distinctive theories along with their alleged facts. All bodies, for instance, are supposed to have perception. The imagination is held capable of affecting physical processes like brewing and butter-making. Nor are these magico-alchemical influences confined to the *Sylva*. They exist also in the most carefully considered works. Thus the transmutation of metals is with Bacon a dominant theme, even his atomism being modified in favour of this belief. Bodies are not consistently thought of as atomic structures but rather as made up 'of simple natures' – gold, for instance, of yellowness, a certain specific weight, ductility, malleability, and so on. He thinks of breaking substances down into simple natures on the analogy of breaking words down into letters. With an alphabet of such simple natures man could re-write Nature's book.

Deeper still, more pervasive, and fundamental to the Baconian philosophy is the doctrine of knowledge as power, a doctrine which, indeed, involves a new definition of man. Man is no longer, as in the philosophy of the Greeks, the rational animal. The first aphorism of *Novum Organum* runs: 'Man, the servant and interpreter of nature, does and understands just so much as he has discerned concerning the order of nature by practice or theory; he neither knows nor can do more.'[1] Now it is again to the magico-alchemical tradition that the notion of man as the servant and interpreter of nature

---

1. The phrase here rendered 'practice or theory' is in the Latin *re vel mente*. The word *re* is unclear. The same sentence is repeated verbatim in *Distributio Operis* with the substitution of *opere* for *re*. *Opere vel mente* restores perfect balance to the sense. A. Lipschutz, *Tres Medicos Contemporaneos*, Buenos Aires, 1958, p. 198, is surely right in treating *re* as a mistake of transcription.

belongs. So profound was Bacon's debt to the tradition he scornfully rejects.

Fully to understand the situation in which Bacon found himself we must look a little closer at the mental history of Europe. Throughout the Middle Ages two world-views had contended with one another. Christianity, as we have already had occasion to remark, had begun in the expectation of the near end of the natural order of things. The emphasis on eschatological doctrine was heavy. For theology, and for the philosophy that was its hand-maid, this world was but a passing show. Yet other-worldliness did not reign unchallenged. In the magico-alchemical tradition, deriving from pre-Christian origins, this world existed in its own right. The alchemists and the magicians, whatever their other follies, kept alive a belief in the reality of the natural world and in the capacity of man to work great changes in nature by natural means. With them the *magnalia Dei* did not exclude the possibility of *magnalia naturae*. Their tradition, surviving only on the fringe of official Christian thought, spoke of mighty works of nature which had nothing to do with the supernatural miracles of the saints. Already in the thirteenth century Roger Bacon had fought for the inclusion of magic within the closed circle of Christian disciplines. With the advent of the Renaissance, which might in one aspect be described as the dwindling of other-worldliness and the growth of belief in this world, alchemists and magicians appeared to be in the van of progress and their disciplines made bolder claims for recognition. Cornelius Agrippa marvelled that the ancient tradition of magic should be decried by the Church, and he had strong supporters within its fold. Magic, at least, had one root of modern science in it, belief in nature. 'The operations of magic proceed from nature and are done in accordance with nature', wrote Agrippa. Della Porta, Paracelsus, Cardan, all said the same. Here, then, were champions of nature at grips with scholastic philosophy. What more did Bacon want? Why could he not stoutly declare himself a follower of the tradition to which he owed much and with which he seemed to side? Why, above all, should scholasticism and magic appear side by side in his writings as the two giants he had to slay before he could liberate human knowledge and set it on the true path?

The reasons for his condemnation of alchemy and magic are clearly and sufficiently set forth in the writings translated in this book. They constitute an essential part of Bacon's contribution to science and may be briefly summarised:

(1) The operations of magicians and alchemists are confined to a narrow

range of experience and produce but few effects, and those of a nature to rouse wonder rather than serve any useful purpose.

(2) The theory on which their operations rests is entangled in an obscure, ancient and partly auricular tradition which has given free rein to gross imposture.

(3) The spirit in which they carry out their operations is corrupted by vain-glory and self-seeking.

(4) The practitioners believe themselves to be a privileged class of *illuminati*, whose knowledge is above the reach of ordinary men and must be kept from them by the deliberate adoption of an obscure and enigmatic style. The curious student could find the justification of all these grave charges by studying the first English translation of Agrippa's book.[1] This translation, belonging to the middle of the seventeenth century, shows the hold magic still had on an educated public on the eve of the foundation of the Royal Society.

From this examination it emerges that Bacon's condemnation of magic and alchemy, like his condemnation of scholasticism, rested on moral as well as intellectual grounds. Against the barrenness and pretentiousness of both traditions, he sought to set up the claims of an activity both useful and humble, which he found in the mechanical arts. 'In the sweat of thy brow shalt thou eat bread.' That had always been the basis of human society and must form the starting-point for future advance. As Bacon had learned from Agricola the social significance of mining and metallurgy, so from Palissy he had learned the dependence of society on a wide range of other crafts. He generalised the lesson in his own words. 'The difference between civilised men and savages', he wrote, 'is almost as great as that between gods and men; and this difference arises not from soil, not from climate, not from race, but from the arts.'[2] His proposal then was that the accumulated experience of humanity in the practical arts should be first gathered and then winnowed. It should be collected according to the particular crafts and then sorted and rearranged to provide material for the different sciences. It is a complete mistake to think that he put the craftsman on the same level as the scientist. The purpose of the whole operation was to facilitate the emergence of science out of craft knowledge. The scientist, however, must be humble

---

1. *Three Books of Occult Philosophy*, written by Henry Cornelius Agrippa of Nettesheim, Counsellor to Charles the Fifth, Emperor of Germany, and Judge of the Prerogative Court. Translated out of the Latin into the English tongue. By J. F., London, 1651.
2. Sp. I, 222 (IV, 114).

enough to understand that no degree of cleverness could compensate for the ignorance of particular facts. The most attractive theories must abide the test of experiment. But the new knowledge, when gained, would be fed back into the industrial life of the nation.

This was no small task, as Bacon well knew. It was King's business. It could not be left to the monk in his cloister, the alchemist's furnace, the rich nobleman's curiosity, or the workshop of the artisan. It required to be taken under the wing of the government. It must enjoy the blessing of the Church and the approval of the universities. It needed the provision of new institutions adapted to its special ends and adequately equipped and financed. It should be organised as a democratic, co-operative enterprise intended for the public good and seen to be so. It invited international co-operation as a thing of concern for all mankind. For it was not simply an addition to knowledge but the inauguration of a new way of life, the great instauration of man's dominion over the universe.

Such in practical terms was the plan. But for Bacon himself it was also a burning vision, seen in his boyhood, cherished throughout life, worked for with 'the wisdom of the serpent' in enforced patience through endless delays amidst men who for the most part could not share it, but retaining its authority to the end. Let him, then, describe it in his own words. They belong to the seventeenth century and much water has flowed under the bridge since a scientist could express his meaning in precisely these words and these images. But if we want to come close to Bacon we must come close to him as he was, not as the historian with a twentieth-century mind would refashion him and rephrase his thoughts. We need to recapture his faith, and that can still be felt through the antiquated vesture in which it is clothed. It adds to the force of his words that they were written as a part of his *Preface* to *The History of Winds* in 1623, three years before his death. It was what the old man felt about the winds, and how they might be made serviceable to man, that prompted this extraordinary burst of prophetic eloquence: for the uniqueness of his personality lay in his vision of the relation of man to nature, as, indeed, his friend George Herbert perceived, who thought of him as –

> Mundique et animarum sacerdos unicus
> (The alone only priest of nature and men's souls).

Here are the words: 'Wherefore, if there be any humility towards the Creator, if there be any praise and reverence towards his works: if there be any charity towards men, and zeal to lessen human wants and sufferings;

if there be any love of truth in natural things, any hatred of darkness, any desire to purify the understanding; men are to be entreated again and again that they should dismiss for a while, or at least put aside, those inconstant and preposterous philosophies, which prefer theses to hypotheses, have led experience captive, and triumphed over the works of God; that they should humbly and with a certain reverence draw near to the book of Creation; that they should there make a stay, that on it they should meditate, and that then washed and clean they should in chastity and integrity turn them from opinion. This is that speech and language which has gone out to all the ends of the earth, and has not suffered the confusion of Babel; this men must learn, and, resuming their youth, they must become again as little children and deign to take its alphabet into their hands.'[1]

1. Sp. II, 14–15.

PART TWO

TRANSLATIONS

NOTE ON THE LATIN TEXTS AND THE METHOD OF
TRANSLATION

The translation is based on the texts as printed by Spedding. *T.P.M.*
and *C. et V.* were first printed by Gruter in 1653, *R.Ph.* by Stephen in
1734. The date of composition of *T.P.M.* has been in dispute. I agree
with the arguments of Anderson and Rossi that it cannot be later than
1603. But how much earlier was it? Anderson wishes to place it very
early as a youthful indiscretion. Rossi sees that it is too close to the
heart of Bacon's mature thought to be dismissed in this way, but still
calls it juvenile. Both have overlooked the fact that it mentions the
death of Peter Severinus, which took place on 28th August, 1602. It
was therefore written when Bacon was forty-one or forty-two.

As regards the method of translation, I have found as Anne Bacon
did with Bishop Jewel and as Spedding did with Bacon himself, that
the thought in the Latin is so embedded in the syntax that a word for
word translation is a mere betrayal. But I have laboured to carry the
exact sense into English idiom.

B.F.

The Masculine Birth of Time

OR

THE GREAT INSTAURATION OF
THE DOMINION OF MAN
OVER THE UNIVERSE

TO GOD THE FATHER

God the Word, God the Spirit, we pour out our humble
and burning prayers, that mindful of the miseries of the
human race and this our mortal pilgrimage in which we
wear out evil days and few, they would send down upon
us new streams from the fountains of their mercy for the
relief of our distress; and this too we would ask, that our
human interests may not stand in the way of the divine, nor
from the unlocking of the paths of sense and the enkindling
of a greater light in nature may any unbelief or darkness
arise in our minds to shut out the knowledge of the divine
mysteries; but rather that the intellect made clean and pure
from all vain fancies, and subjecting itself in voluntary submission to the divine oracles, may render to faith the things
that belong to faith.

The Masculine Birth of Time

OR

THREE BOOKS ON THE
INTERPRETATION OF NATURE

BOOK 1. Polishing and Direction of the Mind
BOOK 2. The Light of Nature or Formula of Interpretation
BOOK 3. Nature Illuminated, or The Truth of Things[1]

CHAPTER ONE

The Legitimate Mode of handing on the Torch of Science[2]

I find, my son, that many men, whether in publishing or concealing the knowledge of nature they think they have won, fall far short of a proper standard of honour or duty. Others again, men of excellent character but poor understanding, produce, through no fault of their own, the same harmful result. What they lack is any art or precepts to guide them in putting their knowledge before the public. Do not suppose, however, that my purpose is to raise a lament about this failure, be it the consequence of malice or incompetence on the part of those whose business it is to maintain the tradition of the sciences. There would, of course, be excuse for anger if

1. The promise of three books makes plain that what follows is only a fragment.
2. The *form* of this writing (a monologue addressed by an older man in authority to a younger man whom he calls 'son') finds its explanation in *De Augmentis VI*, 2 (Sp. IV, 449). There Bacon distinguishes the *magistral* from the *initiative* method of transmitting knowledge. 'The one transmits knowledge to the crowd of learners, the other to the sons, as it were, of science. The end of the one is the use of knowledges as they now are, of the other the continuation and progression of them.'

by their lack of skill they broke the force of any weighty matter. In fact the incompetence of their teaching must be ascribed to the worthlessness of their knowledge.

I for my part have set my face in the opposite direction. My intention is to impart to you, not the figments of my own brain, nor the shadows thrown by words, nor a mixture of religion and science, nor a few commonplace observations or notorious experiments tricked out to make a composition as fanciful as a stage-play. No; I am come in very truth leading to you Nature with all her children to bind her to your service and make her your slave. Does it seem to you then that I bear in my hands a subject of instruction which I can risk defiling by any fault in my handling of it, whether springing from pretence or incompetence? So may it go with me, my son; so may I succeed in my only earthly wish, namely to stretch the deplorably narrow limits of man's dominion over the universe to their promised bounds; as I shall hand on to you, with the most loyal faith, out of the profoundest care for the future of which I am capable, after prolonged examination both of the state of nature and the state of the human mind, by the most legitimate method, the instruction I have to convey.

But what, you ask, is this legitimate method. Please drop all arts and subterfuges, you say, and put the matter plainly before us, so that we may use our own judgment. Would to God, my dear boy, that your situation was such that this could be done. But do you suppose, when all the approaches and entrances to men's minds are beset and blocked by the most obscure idols – idols deeply implanted and, as it were, burned in – that any clean and polished surface remains in the mirror of the mind on which the genuine natural light of things can fall? A new method must be found for quiet entry into minds so choked and overgrown. Frenzied men are exacerbated by violent opposition but may be beguiled by art. This gives us a hint how we should proceed in this universal madness. Do you really think it is easy to provide the favourable conditions required for the legitimate passing on of knowledge? The method must be mild and afford no occasion of error. It must have in it an inherent power of winning support and a vital principle which will stand up against the ravages of time, so that the tradition of science may mature and spread like some lively vigorous vine. Then also science must be such as to select her followers, who must be worthy to be adopted into her family. This is what must be provided. Whether I can manage it or not the future must decide.

And now, my son, I do not conceal from you that we must find a way of clearing sham philosophers out of our path. Your philosophers are more fabulous than poets. They debauch our minds. They substitute a false coinage for the true. And worse still are the satellites and parasites of the great ones, the whole mob of professorial teachers. Will not someone recite the formula by which I may devote them all to oblivion? How shall truth be heard, if they maintain the din of their grovelling and inconsequent ratiocinations?

But, now that I think of it, it will be safer to condemn them one by one by name; for their authority is great and if not named they may be thought to be excepted. Nor would I have anyone suppose, seeing the hatred and fury with which they wage their internecine strife, that I have come to lend my support to one side or the other in this battle of ghosts and shadows. Come, then, let Aristotle be summoned to the bar, that worst of sophists[1] stupified by his own unprofitable subtlety, the cheap dupe of words. Just when the human mind, borne thither by some favouring gale, had found rest in a little truth, this man presumed to cast the closest fetters on our understandings. He composed an art or manual of madness and made us slaves of words. Nay more, it was in his bosom that were bred and nurtured those crafty triflers, who turned themselves away from the perambulation of our globe and from the light of nature and of history; who from the pliant material provided by his precepts and propositions, and relying on the restless agitation of their own wit, spun out for us the countless quibbles of the Schools. But he, their dictator, is more to blame than they. He still moved in the daylight of honest research when he fetched up his darksome idols from some subterranean cave, and over such observation of particulars as had been made spun as it were spiders' webs which he would have us accept as causal bonds, though they have no strength nor worth.

In our modern age the same sort of webs have been spun with great industry by Jerome Cardan, who, like Aristotle, is at variance with facts and with himself.

Now, son, when I bring this charge against Aristotle you must not suppose me to be in league with that recent rebel against him, Peter Ramus. I

1. In what sense he classed Aristotle, and Plato, among the Sophists Bacon explains in *The Refutation of Philosophies* (see p. 111).

have nothing in common with that hide-out of ignorance, that pestilent book-worm, that begetter of handy manuals. Any facts he gets hold of and begins to squeeze in the rack of his summary method soon lose their truth, which oozes or skips away, leaving him to garner only dry and barren trifles. Aquinas, Scotus, and their followers out of their unrealities created a varied world; Ramus out of the real world made a desert. Though that was the character of the man he has the effrontery to prate of human utilities. I rate him below the sophists. So let us have done with these gentlemen.

Let Plato next be summoned to the bar, that mocking wit, that swelling poet, that deluded theologian. Your philosophy, Plato, was but scraps of borrowed information polished and strung together. Your wisdom was a sham which you imposed by an affectation of ignorance. By your vague inductions you took men's minds off their guard and weakened their mental sinews. But you had at least the merit of supplying table-talk for men of culture and experience of affairs, even indeed of adding grace and charm to everyday conversation. When, however, you gave out the falsehood that truth is, as it were, the native inhabitant of the human mind and need not come in from outside to take up its abode there; when you turned our minds away from observation, away from things, to which it is impossible we should ever be sufficiently respectful and attentive; when you taught us to turn our mind's eye inward and grovel before our own blind and confused idols under the name of contemplative philosophy; then truly you dealt us a mortal blow. Nor should it be forgotten that you were guilty of no less a sin when you deified your folly and presumed to shore up your contemptible thoughts with the prop of religion.

It is a lesser evil that you became the parent of the writing confraternity, and that by your guidance and under your auspices many a man, seduced by the desire for literary renown and satisfied with a popular and easily acquired knowledge of nature, damaged the ideal of a stricter and more thorough investigation of the truth. Examples are Marcus Cicero, Annaeus Seneca, Plutarch of Chaeronea, and many another of lesser worth.

Now let us turn to the physicians. Is that Galen I see there, the narrow-minded Galen, who deserted the path of experience and took to spinning idle theories of causation? You there, Galen, are you the man who rescued from infamy the ignorance and idleness of the medical profession? Was it you who lodged the profession in a safe shelter by setting such limits to the art and duty of medicine as should suit their sloth? Did you take it upon you to pronounce this disease incurable, and that, cutting short the patient's hopes and the physician's labours? Baleful Star![1] Plague of the human race! You would have us believe that only Nature can produce a true compound. You snatch at the notion that the heat of the sun and the heat of fire are different things and parade this opinion with the malicious intention of lessening human power wherever you can and of bolstering up ignorance to all eternity through despair of any improvement. The concession I make to your worthlessness is that I shall not detain you longer. But stay a moment. Do not forget to take your Arabian confederates with you, those compounders of drugs who have managed to combine with a theoretical folly to match the best of you a more copious talent in hoaxing, not healing, the public with their bogus remedies.

Take with you too the perfunctory mob of modern physicians. Nomenclator, supply me with their names. What? Their names are not important enough for you to remember? True they are worthless fellows, but for my part I recognise certain ranks and grades among them, and hold the worst and most contemptible to be those who win general applause for the eloquence and orderliness of their writings while confining the whole art of medicine within the narrow bounds of their hair-splitting method. Fernel is one of these. Less noxious are those who exhibit a greater variety and propriety of experimental material, even if diluted and drowned in a flood of stupid argumentation. An example is Arnoldus de Villa Nova.

But there on the other side I see the Alchemists arrayed, Paracelsus among them conspicuous for his braggart air. His presumption calls for a particular reproof. I have been taking to task people who peddle falsehoods; your stock in trade is portents. In meteorology, O you rival of Epicurus, what drunken oracles do you not pour forth! Indeed, Epicurus, like a man dropping off to sleep or with his attention fixed on something else, utters words at random. But your utterances are too silly to be random. You seek out the most absurd authorities to swear allegiance to. But you do not restrict yourself to meteorology. You have a passion for taking your idols in pairs and dreaming up mutual imitations, correspondences, parallelisms, between the products of your elements. As for man, you have made him into a pantomime.[2] Who can fail to wonder at the distinctions, products of your own imagination, by which you have torn asunder the unity of nature? It is easier to put up with

1. The Latin here is O Canicula!, and the reference is to the Dog-star which heralded the advent of the season of fevers.

2. An allusion to the doctrine of macrocosm and microcosm, which sees all sorts of correspondences between man and the universe.

Galen speculating on his elements than with you engaged in tricking out your own fancies. He tried to study the hidden properties of things, you their obvious and superficial qualities. It is we who deserve pity for spending our time in the midst of such distasteful trivialities. With what misplaced zeal this man, skilled in all the arts of imposture, seeks to impose upon us his triad of first principles,[1] though admittedly this scheme is not utterly useless and does bear some relation to things.

But now hear graver charges. By mixing the divine with the natural, the profane with the sacred, heresies with mythology, you have corrupted, O you sacrilegious impostor, both human and religious truth. The light of nature, whose holy name is ever on your lips, you have not merely hidden, like the Sophists, but extinguished. They deserted experience, you have betrayed it. The evidence drawn from things is like a mask cloaking reality and needs careful sifting; you subjected it to a pre-ordained scheme of interpretation. Where you ought to have tried to calculate motions you grasped at the elusive, protean, nature of substances and thus polluted the springs of knowledge and left the human mind stripped of its aids. When the obscurities and delays involved in experimental research were such that the Sophists dodged them and the Empirics were unequal to them, you added fresh obscurities and adventitious delays. It is therefore quite untrue that you followed, or knew, the lead of experience. Nay, even the blind greed of the Magicians you stimulated to the utmost of your powers, your only check on their inordinate thoughts being hope, and on their inordinate hope being promises. You are at once the creator and the creature of imposture.

Only one of your followers do I grudge you, namely Peter Severinus, a man too good to die in the toils of such folly.[2] You, Paracelsus, adopted son of the family of asses, owe him a heavy debt. He took over your brayings and by the tuneful modulations and pleasant inflexions of his voice made sweet harmony of them, transforming your destestable falsehoods into delectable fables. So I find it in my heart to forgive you, Peter Severinus, if, wearying of the teaching of the Sophists, which had not only ceased to be

---

1. Salt, sulphur, mercury.

2. The little known Peter Severinus, so warmly praised by Bacon, was born at Ripon in Denmark in 1542 and died in 1602. Bacon's choice of phrase suggests that he was already dead (perhaps recently dead) when these words were written. If so, this is important evidence for the date of *Temporis Partus Masculus* (cf. Sp. 1, 564 with Ellis's note). I should be prepared to take the word *immoriatur* in a figurative sense were it not for the further suggestion at the end of the paragraph that Severinus was indeed untimely dead. This was in fact the case. He had just been nominated to a professorial chair at Copenhagen which he did not live to occupy.

productive of works but had come to make an explicit profession of despair, you gallantly sought a fresh foundation for our crumbling fortunes. When you came across these doctrines of Paracelsus, recommending themselves by their noisy trumpeting, the cunning of their obscurity, their religious affiliations, and other specious allures, with one impulsive leap you surrendered yourself to what turned out to be not sources of true knowledge but empty delusions. You would have been well and truly advised if your revolt from ingenious paradoxes had taken you instead to nature's laws, which would have offered you a shorter path to knowledge and a longer lease of life.

All the other Alchemists, I notice, have been struck dumb by the judgment passed on Paracelsus. Of course they recognise his opinions as their own, though he rather promulgated them than established them, relying on his arrogance to lend them strength; for he lacked the ancient discipline. These men, in fact, formed a sort of confederacy to back up one another's lies. Thus they recklessly excited extravagant hopes, and if, in the course of their devious wanderings through the jungle of experience, they now and then lighted on something useful, this was by good luck rather than good guidance. For being faithful disciples of the furnace, they never got beyond their art. Like the dainty lad who found a plank on the beach and was seized with the desire to build a ship, so these charcoal-burners on the foundation of a handful of experiments in distillation presumed to found a philosophy, dominated throughout by their grotesque idols of 'separations' and 'liberations.' But I do not put them all in the same class. There is among them a valuable group, not utterly devoted to their theories, which tries, by subtle applications of mechanics, to extend the range of discoveries. Such a one was Roger Bacon. Opposed to them is the criminal and accursed type, for ever canvassing for applause on the strength of their theories, and roping in religion, hope, and imposture to support their cause. Isaac Holland is one of these, like most Alchemists.

Now it is the turn of Hippocrates to appear, that product and puffer of ancient wisdom.[1] Who would not laugh to see Galen and Paracelsus running to take shelter under his authority – under what the proverb calls the shadow of an ass? That fellow has the appearance of maintaining a steady gaze at experience. Too steady! His eyes never shift. They follow nothing. They are sunk in stupor. Then, still but half awake, he snatches up a few idols –

1. This seems to be an allusion to the work *On Ancient Medicine* which introduces the Hippocratic corpus. If so Bacon has been singularly blind to one of the chief pearls of scientific literature.

not the monstrous idols of the great speculative thinkers, but a slim and elegant variety which haunts the surface of science. These he swallows, and swollen with this diet, half scientist and half sophist, protecting himself according to the fashion of his age by an oracular brevity, after long delay he brings out a few maxims, which Galen and Paracelsus take for oracles and quarrel with one another for the honour of interpreting. But in truth the oracle is dumb. He utters nothing but a few sophisms sheltered from correction by their curt ambiguity, or a few peasants' remedies made to sound imposing.

The closest follower of this man's teachings, which were not wicked but merely useless, was, according to the general opinion, Cornelius Celsus, a sophist of a serious kind, devoted to a moderate form of research, concerned to introduce a certain moral control over the advance of science. He pruned the luxuriance of error, but could not nip it in the bud.[1]

The truth of all I have said about these men is undeniable. But I can see, my son, that you want to ask me a question. You want to know whether perhaps, as does happen, it is the inferior writers who have come down to us. You would remind me that it is the condition of science that it is subject to popular opinion. Has not the river of time carried down to us the light and windy and sunk the solid and weighty? What of those old trackers-down of truth? What of Heraclitus, Democritus, Pythagoras, Anaxagoras, Empedocles, and the rest, known to us only through the writings of others? Finally you would wish to know what I think may be hidden behind the silence and the reserve of antiquity.

My son, I shall answer you in my usual way, that is, in accordance with your best interests. I do acknowledge a broken light or two from antiquity (I speak of their discoveries, not of their books); and these broken lights I take rather as proofs of industry and native wit than of any developed science. But as for the writings which have vanished without trace, I know your modesty well enough to be assured that you will not misunderstand me if I suggest that this hunting after guesses is a wearisome business and that it would not be a proper thing for me, who am preparing things useful for the future of the human race, to bury myself in the study of ancient literature.

Nevertheless it is important to understand how the present is like a seer with two faces, one looking towards the future, the other towards the past.

1. In speaking of a moral restraint on scientific progress Bacon probably has in mind the criticism advanced by Celsus on the alleged use by the Alexandrian physicians, Herophilus and Erasistratus, of condemned criminals for human vivisection.

Accordingly I have decided to prepare for your instruction tables of both ages, containing not only the past course and progress of science but also anticipations of things to come. The nature of these tables you could not conjecture before you see them. A genuine anticipation of them is beyond your scope, nor would you even be aware of the lack of it unless it were put into your hands. It is a compliment reserved to some of the choicer spirits among you whom I hope to win thereby. But generally speaking science is to be sought from the light of nature, not from the darkness of antiquity. It matters not what has been done; our business is to see what can be done. If a kingdom won in victorious fighting were offered to you, would you refuse it unless you had followed up the clues of ancient genealogies to prove that your ancestors had held it before? So much for the remote fastnesses of antiquity.[1]

Now about those heads of schools you mentioned judgment is easy. Unity is the hall-mark of truth, and the variety of their opinions is proof of error. In fact, had not political conditions and prospects put an end to these mental voyages, many another coast of error would have been visited by those mariners. For the island of truth is lapped by a mighty ocean in which many intellects will still be wrecked by the gales of illusion. Nay, it was only yesterday that Bernardinus Telesius mounted the rostrum and staged a new comedy, which was neither well received nor well conceived. Then there are the ingenious contrivers of eccentrics and epicycles on the one hand, and those charioteers of the earth on the other. Do you not observe, son, how both sides delight to support their contrary opinions with the same phenomena? It is the same with the cosmologists. I will suggest a parallel which will explain the universal failure. Take a man who understands only his own vernacular. Put into his hands a writing in an unknown tongue. He picks out a few words here and there which sound like, or are spelled like, words in his own tongue. With complete confidence he jumps to the conclusion that their meaning is the same, though as a rule this is very far from true. Then, on the basis of this resemblance, he proceeds to guess the sense of the rest of the document with great mental exertion and equal licence. This is a true image of these interpreters of nature. For each man brings his own idols – I am not now speaking of those of the stage, but particularly of those of the market-place and the cave – and applies them, like his own vernacular, to

---

1. The last three paragraphs make clear that the idea of a science of nature 'hidden behind the silence and the reserve of antiquity' has already entered Bacon's mind, but he is not yet prepared to take it seriously.

the interpretation of nature, snatching at any facts which fit in with his pre-conceptions and forcing everything else into harmony with them.

But now I must recollect myself and do penance, for though my purpose was only to discredit it yet I have been handling what is unholy and unclean. What I have said against them all has been less than their monstrous guilt deserved. You very likely do not understand my refutation of them. You are sure that the charges I have levelled against them are mere abuse. But this is not so. Do not confuse me with Velleius in Cicero's dialogue, that literary declaimer who touches only the surface of an opinion and rejects it without destroying it, nor with the modern Agrippa, who is not fit to be named a controversialist, but a trivial buffoon, relying on distortion and ridicule. It is bad luck for me that, for lack of men, I must compare myself with brute beasts. But when you have had time to reflect you will see things differently. You will admire beneath the veil of abuse the spirit that has animated my attack. You will observe the skill with which I have packed every word with meaning and the accuracy with which I have launched my shafts straight into their hidden sores. Those whom I incriminate share a common guilt and might well have been confounded in a common accusation; but I have been at pains to frame an indictment appropriate to each individual and particu-larising his chief offence.

The fact is, my son, that the human mind in studying nature becomes big under the impact of things and brings forth a teeming brood of errors. Aristotle stands for the tallest growth of one kind of error, Plato of another, and so on for the rest. Now, you would like me to confute them individually. But verily that would be to sin on the grand scale against the golden future of the human race, to sacrifice its promise of dominion by turning aside to attack transitory shadows. The need is to set up in the midst one bright and radiant light of truth, shedding its beams in all directions and dispelling all errors in a moment. It is pointless to light pale candles and carry them about to every nook and cranny of error and falsehood. I would have you learn to hate that for which you ask. Believe me, it is to sin against the light.

But again I hear you ask: Can everything taught by all these men be vain and false? My son, it is not a question of ignorance but of ill-luck, for they lack method and are monstrously deceived.[1] Everybody stumbles on some truth sooner or later. Heraclitus said the mistake was to seek knowledge, not

1. The Latin here is obscure through brevity. The meaning becomes clear by comparison with a passage in *Thoughts and Conclusions* where the train of thought is repeated (Sp. III, 609; and p. 91 of this book).

in the common world but in the private world of each man. This was a prosperous omen at the very outset of philosophy. Democritus attributed to nature immense variety and infinite succession, thus setting himself apart from almost all other philosophers, who were prisoners of their times and slaves of fashion. This was a genuine contribution to philosophy. By his stand he destroyed two falsehoods by knocking their heads together and opened up a middle path to truth. The number philosophy of Pythagoras I hold to be full of promise. I commend the Indian Dindamis for his definition of custom as 'anti-nature.' I am content to listen to Epicurus when he disputes the doctrine of final causes, even though he does it in an elementary and bookish way. I even find entertainment in Pyrrho and the Academics, though they waver from one side to the other like an orator speaking from a boat, and behave towards their idols like moody lovers who rail at their sweethearts but never leave them. How should I not? For, while other philosophers follow straight after their idols, these fellows are led round and round in circles, which is more diverting. Lastly, take Paracelsus and Severinus. When they lift up their voices and summon men to gather together in honour of Experience, then they are the right criers for me. But what follows? That they are in possession of the truth? Far from it. Why, even country bumpkins have proverbs which are apt expressions of truth. A pig might print the letter A with its snout in the mud, but you would not on that account expect it to go on to compose a tragedy. That kind of truth which is deduced from scientific analogy is very different from a mere coincidence between experience and some baseless hypothesis. Genuine truth is uniform and self-reproducing. Lucky hits are contradictory and solitary. This holds good both for truth and works. If gunpowder had been discovered, not by good luck but by good guidance, it would not have stood alone but been accompanied by a host of noble inventions of a kindred sort. I warn you, then, not to be deceived by the chance coincidence in some point of their theories with my, or rather nature's, truth. Do not judge too well of them or too ill of me. Wait and you will see from their ignorance in other matters that they have not based their findings on scientific analogy.

Do you still ask me whether all those many pages they have written should be used to wrap up incense and odours? I would not say that. There does remain for some time some use for them, limited indeed and different from that for which they were intended, but still some use. It is worth noting too that many writings of lesser renown are more serviceable. The ethics of Plato and Aristotle are much admired; but the pages of Tacitus breathe a

Thoughts and Conclusions

ON

THE INTERPRETATION OF NATURE OR
A SCIENCE PRODUCTIVE OF WORKS

(1. The imperfections of the practical sciences of Nature)[1]

Francis Bacon thought thus: The science in the possession of which the human race continues up to the present day does not attain to certainty or greatness of effects. The doctors pronounce many diseases incurable, and in their treatment of the rest often err and fail. The alchemists grow old and die in the embraces of their illusion. The achievements of the magicians are unsure and fruitless. The mechanical arts draw little light from philosophy, though they do gradually enlarge the humble web woven by experience. Chance without doubt is a useful originator of things, but scatters her blessings on mankind only after tedious and tortuous wanderings.

Hence he drew three conclusions: The human discoveries we now enjoy should rank as quite imperfect and undeveloped. In the present state of the sciences new discoveries can be expected only after the lapse of centuries. The discoveries men have up to now achieved cannot be credited to philosophy.

(2. The wrong attitude of men towards the Sciences)

He thought also as follows: In the existing narrowness of men's fortunes what is most deplorable for the present and ominous for the future is that men, against their own interests, try to protect their ignorance from its due ignominy, and to make do with the little they have. The *Medical Practitioner*, in addition to the particular reserves incidental to the practice of his art (on which he relies for the safeguarding of its reputation), summons also to his aid a certain comprehensive reserve as to the possibilities of his art as a whole. That is to say, he seeks to transform the present limitations of his art into a permanent reproach against nature and whatever his art cannot achieve he artfully declares to be impossible in nature. And of course his art escapes condemnation in a court where it is itself the judge. *Philosophy* too, from which the art of medicine has been carved, nourishes in its bosom certain pet

---

1. The numbering of the sections and their titles are supplied by the translator.

73

theories, which, if critically examined, amount to this, that nothing really great, no effective control over nature, can be won by human ingenuity or art. This is the source of such sayings as that the heat of the sun is different in kind from the heat of fire; or that man can only juxtapose things and must leave it to nature to combine them. But, if these propositions be looked into, their effect is found to be a mischievous limitation of human power, a deliberately contrived mood of despair, which rejects not only the auguries of hope but the windfalls of experience and hamstrings the promptings and sinews of all enterprise. What the philosophers are concerned with is that their art should be held perfect. They want their vainglorious and ruinous boast, that whatever has not yet been discovered is indiscoverable, to pass still for true. The *Alchemist*, on the other hand, in order to exalt the reputation of his art, shifts the blame for his failure on to his own short-comings. He misunderstood (so he alleges) the meaning of some term or passage and he turns his attention again to the superficial whisperings of an oral tradition. Or he slipped up (so he says) in the minutiæ of his practice, made a mistake in the proportions or weights. Thus he repeats his experiments to infinity under more favourable auspices this time (so he hopes); and, if he ever does stumble in the course of his bewildering experiments on some result superficially novel or of moderate utility, he feasts his mind on such pledges of success, exaggerates them, spreads the report of them, and continues to subsist on hope. The *Magician*, for his part, when he manages (according to his understanding of the matter) to produce some supernatural effect, thinking that he has now got nature in his power, gives wings to his imagination, loses his sense of proportion, and supposes that there is nothing any longer to which he may not aspire. He fails to notice that there is common to all nations and ages a certain narrow range of operations within which Magic and Superstition produce their delusive effects. As for the *Mechanic*, he is apt to think himself as among the great inventors, if he has had the good luck to give a finer finish or enhanced elegance to some old invention, to combine in one what was previously separate, to make a fruitful application to practice of something already known, or to reproduce a familiar model on a bigger or smaller scale.

From these considerations Bacon concluded: That men either despise invention as a waste of effort; or, if they believe that splendid discoveries have been made, suppose the knowledge of them to be wrapt up in jealous silence by the few; or descend to the level of calling every petty addition or improvement to the practice of the crafts a new invention. The net result is the abandonment of the noble task of adding by open and steady toil to the sum of inventions worthy of the human race.

(3. *Imagined plenty the cause of real poverty*)

He thought also: When men survey the variety of operations and the elaborate apparatus made available by the mechanical arts for the uses of civilisation, they are inclined rather to marvel at the wealth of man than to appreciate his poverty. They fall into this mistake because they fail to see that the original operations of nature observed by man, which form, as it were, the soul or First Mover of all that admired variety, are really neither many nor fetched from any great depth. All the rest depends only on human patience and the deft and regulated movement of hand or tool. Indeed, so far as this last point is concerned, a workshop is wonderfully like a library; for a library also exhibits a wonderful variety of books, but, if you look closer, you find only infinite repetition, new in the manner but not in the substance.

The conclusion: Imagined plenty is one of the causes of real poverty. Both craft knowledge and book learning look great but on examination are found to be small.

(4. *The Immobility of the Sciences*)

Another reflection: The branches of knowledge we possess are presented with too much pretension and show. They are dressed up for the public view in such a way as to suggest that the individual arts are one and all perfected in every part and brought to their final development. Their methodical treatment and their sub-divisions suggest that everything that could fall under the subject is already included. Branches of knowledge which are poorly nourished and lacking in vital sap make a show of presenting a complete whole, and a few treatises, not always even selected from the best authors, come to be accepted as complete and adequate accounts of their subjects. Yet the most ancient searchers after truth, who were more reliable, preferred to compress into aphorisms, or brief disconnected unmethodical sentences, the knowledge they had gathered from the observation of nature and thought worth preserving. This method of presentation was less misleading. It gave a bare outline of their discoveries and left obvious blanks where no discoveries had been made. It was a stimulating method which made their readers think and judge for themselves. But nowadays the sciences are presented in such a way as to enslave belief instead of provoking criticism; the intervention of a blighting authority precludes fruitful research. Consequently the whole scientific process has become a succession of teachers and pupils and not of inventors and improvers of inventions. Inevitably the sciences have become stuck in their tracks and cannot be moved forward. This has been the state of affairs now for many centuries. An answer remains an answer and a problem a problem, and no progress is made.

The conclusion: Pillars have been erected beyond which progress is forbidden, and there is no ground for surprise that man does not achieve an end which he neither hopes nor desires.

(5. *The goal of the Sciences is wrongly set*)

Another thought: What was said above, about men's despair of knowledge or their arrogant display of it, is to take them too seriously. Most of those engaged in it are interested in something else. They seek only mental satisfaction, or a lucrative profession, or some support and ornament for their renown. But if these are taken to be the ends of the sciences, not only do men not strive to augment the sum of knowledge, but all they look for is to extract from it the little required for their particular use. And if among the numerous scientists there be one who seeks knowledge with an honest heart and for its own sake, he will be found to aim at *variety* rather than *verity*. Even if he turns out an exceptionally strict seeker after truth, still his verity will be better adapted to give a more *subtle* interpretation of things already known than to elicit new light.[1]

Supposing finally his zeal for knowledge is so enlarged as to include an aspiration after new light, yet the light will be such as to make a brilliant intellectual display from a distance and not to reveal at close quarters remarkable discoveries and inventions.

The conclusion is as before: It is no wonder that the course is not run when the runners turn aside to lesser ends. Indeed, so far as Bacon knows, the goal has never been defined. Simply it is that the human race should be steadily enriched with new works and powers.

(6. *Neglect of Natural Philosophy*)

A further reflection: All the sciences are badly served, but Natural Philosophy worst of all. It has only superficially engaged the attention of men; it has been

---

1. No doubt a reference is intended here to Cardan's *De Varietate Rerum* and his *De Subtilitate Rerum*. Cardan visited King Edward VI in 1552 and thought of dedicating to him his *De Varietate*. The King's early death precluded the fulfilment of the plan.

soon dropped; it has never been seriously cultivated and brought under the plough. Once the Christian faith had been established and received, the majority of men of wit applied themselves to Theology, to which branch of learning the most handsome rewards and generous aids were directed. Furthermore, even in the prechristian age most philosophers devoted themselves to Moral Philosophy, which with the pagans took the place of Theology. In both cases many of the loftiest intellects took to politics and administration, especially during the period of Roman greatness, when the size of the Empire claimed the exertions of many. Natural Philosophy did flourish among the Greeks for a time, but the period was brief. The love of argument and novelties soon put an end to its usefulness. During all those ages up till now no single individual made a profession of Natural Philosophy in the sense of devoting his life to it. To repeat, up till now Natural Philosophy has never engaged the whole time and attention of any man, unless it were of some monk in his cell or some noble in his villa, and not many such examples will be found. Instead Natural Philosophy has been made a sort of bridge or passage to other things. The Great Mother of the Sciences has been reduced to their handmaid. Her function is to tend on medicine and mathematics and give the undeveloped minds of adolescents a preliminary tincture to facilitate their progress in other studies.

What should one conclude? First, having regard to the few who cultivate it, the haste with which they abandon it, and the rawness of their minds, Natural Philosophy is utterly neglected. And what follows on this? What is true of Natural Philosophy is true of all learning. All arts and sciences once severed from this root may perhaps be polished and fitted to some use: they cannot grow.

(7. *Injuries inflicted on Science by Theology*)

He pursued also the following train of thought: In Superstition and in blind immoderate religious zeal Natural Philosophy has found a troublesome and intractable enemy. Among the Greeks those who first suggested to men's untutored minds that thunderbolts and storms had natural causes were condemned for impiety. On the accusation of some of the early Christian fathers Cosmographers, who on clear evidence which no sane man could reject today, claimed that the earth was a sphere and therefore inhabited at the antipodes, fared little better than the Greeks. They were brought to trial for impiety, though they lost only their reputations, not their lives. In our own days discussions concerning nature have been subjected to even harsher constraint by reason of the boldness of the Scholastics and their followers. They have not only done their best to reduce Theology into the form of a manual[1] but have had the temerity to incorporate the disputations and contentious philosophy of Aristotle into the body of religion.

Another example of the same kind of dangerous tendency is that no opinions are in such favour today as those which with solemn pomp seek to celebrate a legal marriage between Theology and Natural Philosophy, that is between Faith and the evidence of the senses, and which charm the minds of men with a pleasing variety of matter while producing a disastrous confusion between the human and the divine.[2] The careful inquirer will find that there is more danger to Natural Philosophy from this specious and ill-matched union than from open hostility. For in this intimate contract only what is already received in Natural Philosophy is included; all fresh growth, additions, improvements are excluded more strictly and obstinately than ever before. In fine every development of philosophy, every new frontier and direction, is regarded by religion with unworthy suspicion and violent contempt.

Others of a simpler turn of mind fear lest any thorough enquiry into nature may transgress permitted bounds. They make the mistake of transferring what is said about divine mysteries (many of which remain under the divine seal) to the hidden things of nature, which are under no interdict. There are those too whose cunning leads them to suppose that, if secondary causes are unknown, everything will be directly referred to the hand and magic wand of God. This they suppose to be of great importance for religion, but in fact they merely seek to please God by a lie. Others, not without warrant in precedent, fear that any change and stir in Natural Philosophy is bound to end in a clash with religion which will bring it to a halt. Some finally even fear that in the enquiry into nature something may come to light which will overthrow religion. Both these fears smack of incredulity and unspiritual wisdom. The latter, indeed, cannot be entertained without impiety.[3]

The conclusion of this meditation is that in opinions of this sort there is much evidence of weakness, malice and instability. Next to the word of God Natural Philosophy is the most certain cure for superstition and the most

1. This is a recurrent complaint with Bacon, who evidently thought the knowledge of God should continue to grow. Bruno, Galileo and Campanella are examples of natural philosophers who suffered harsh constraint.
2. Bacon's target here is the Christian Platonism stemming from Ficino.
3. *Filum labyrinthi* goes into this point at length. Sp. III, 500ff.

approved nutriment of faith. Its rightful station is as the accepted and loyal handmaid of religion, for religion reveals the will of God, Natural Philosophy His power. He was not wrong who said: Ye err being ignorant of the Scriptures and of the power of God,[1] thus linking together knowledge of God's will and meditation on His power by an indissoluble bond. But though this be so, the analysis given above stands unshaken. Among present obstacles to Natural Philosophy zeal without knowledge and blind superstition stand supreme.

(8. *Bad organisation of Cultural Institutions*)

Another train of thought: In the traditions and organisation of Academies, Colleges, and other institutions designed as seats of learning and for the interchange of ideas, everything inimical to the progress of the sciences is to be found. Far the greater number of persons there are concerned primarily with lecturing and in the next place with making a living; and the lectures and other exercises are so managed that the last thing anyone would be likely to entertain is an unfamiliar thought. Anyone who allows himself freedom of enquiry or independence of judgment promptly finds himself isolated. If he survives this, when he comes to choose a career in the world he finds his enthusiasm and non-conformity a great obstacle. For in these places studies are confined to the works of certain authorities; a man who disagrees with them or raises awkward questions is censured as a disturbing and revolutionary influence. Yet to any true discernment it should be clear that there is a distinction between politics and the arts. Fresh light and innovations are not as dangerous in the one case as in the other. In politics even improvements are suspect on account of their power to disturb, for political control rests on authority, assent, reputation, opinion, not on demonstration and on truth. But in the arts and sciences, as in mining for minerals, there ought everywhere to be the bustle of new works and further progress. The distinction is right and necessary.

The conclusion: In actual life the educational policy and administration now in vogue crushes and checks the development and propagation of the sciences.

(9. *Damaging effects of public opinion*)

Another meditation: The whole prevalent climate of opinion raises obstacles on all sides to the advance of science. Most men are unfair to their own age

1. Matthew 22, 29.

and prejudiced in favour of antiquity. They believe that if we were now obliged for the first time to seek what the ancients sought and discovered, we should be quite unequal to the task. They believe too that if a man with confidence in his own mother wit did open up some line of enquiry, he would merely rediscover something already approved by antiquity, or tried, rejected, and deservedly forgotten. Others, out of an absolute contempt for the human race and human understanding, whether in ancient or in modern times, have fallen into an opinion both extravagant and superstitious. They suppose that the first beginnings of the sciences originated with Spirits, and that it is only by Spirits condescending again to consort with men that any new discoveries can be made. Others, whose temper is more strict and sober but whose scepticism is greater still, frankly give up hope of any improvement in the sciences, alleging the obscurity of nature, the shortness of human life, the deceitfulness of the senses, the insecurity of judgment, and the difficulties and endless variety of experiments. According to them only an unsteady and immature mind can entertain hopes of a much better life than we now enjoy; for though the start of the journey is easy, the middle is steep, and the end unsure. They urge that even if discoveries were made they would not be recognised, for they are as dubious of the reception of any great achievement as of its possibility. For sciences are born and brought to maturity in great minds, but the rewarding and honouring of them rests with the people or their leaders, or in any case with men of modest learning. The atomic theory of Democritus they regard as a case in point. Being above men's heads it was received with derision. They do not deny that deeper insights into nature occur from time to time, but since they are as inaccessible to the senses of men as religion itself, after no great lapse of time (unless they are proved and recommended by some obvious and great utility, which up to now has not been the case) they are blown about and extinguished by the wind of popular opinion. For time is like a river which carries down what is light and empty and drowns what is solid and substantial.

Bacon concluded that the obstacles to an improvement in the sciences are not only external and adventitious, but innate and drawn from the very nature of our senses.

(10. *Injuries to Science from limitations of language*)

The nature of words, being vague and ill-defined, is another source of illusion, nay, almost of violence to the human understanding. Words are a kind of currency, which reflect vulgar opinions and preferences, for they combine or distinguish things according to popular notions and acceptations, which are for the most part mistaken or confused. Infants as they learn to speak necessarily drink in a wretched hotch-potch of traditional error. And however much men, as they advance in wisdom and learning, seek by various arts to rescue themselves from this servitude, by inventing new terms, which is difficult, or interposing definitions, which is tedious, yet no matter what they do they can never shake off the yoke. In the keenest discussions verbal controversies continue to arise. Worse still, those faulty meanings of words cast their rays, or stamp their impressions, on the mind itself. They do not only make discourse tedious, but they impair judgment and understanding.

Bacon concluded that among the internal sources of error this defect of language must be reckoned a serious and dangerous one.

(11. *Injury to the reputation of Natural Philosophy through worthless exponents*)

In addition to the difficulties common to all science and branches of learning, Natural Philosophy, especially in its active and operative branch, has its own peculiar prejudices to contend with. It has forfeited much of its reputation and esteem by reason of the irresponsibility and worthlessness of some of its champions. These men, partly because they are credulous and partly because they are impostors, have loaded the human race with promises such as prolongation of life, postponement of old age, relief from pain, repair of natural defects, deceptions of the senses, inhibition or excitement of the emotions, enlightenment of the intellectual faculties, exaltations of mood, transmutation of substances, multiplications of motions as desired, impressions and alterations of the air, divination of future events, visibility of distant events, revelation of hidden things, and so on. What ought we to think of these boasters? Comparing Natural Philosophy with history we might say that there is as great a difference between true science and their vanities as there is between the exploits of Julius Caesar or Alexander the Great and the legends of Amadis of Gaul or Arthur of Britain. Everybody knows that those famous captains accomplished greater things in reality than the shadowy heroes of romance are fabled to have done, and that too by modes of action that have nothing fabulous or miraculous about them. It is not right to refuse faith to a true tradition because faith has often been outraged by fables. It is a fable that Ixion begat centaurs on a cloud while Jove on the real Juno begat Hebe and Vulcan, but from it we may understand God to be the author of the wonderful and divine powers of nature and of art. Admitting the truth of this interpretation and holding it to be a mark of crass stupidity to reject all tradition without distinction of kind, Bacon yet concluded that the path to true knowledge through fictions of this sort has long been closed, or at least narrowed, and that the excess of such vanities is destructive of all greatness of mind.[1]

(12. The Dignity of Experimental Science)

There is in the human mind a certain bias implanted by nature and fostered by opinion and a certain type of training, which has delayed or sidetracked the progress of Natural Philosophy, where it is active or productive of works. This proud pernicious prejudice asserts that the majesty of the human mind is impaired if it employs itself much or long with experiments and particulars, which are subject to the senses and bounded by matter. For such things, it is said, are troublesome to investigate, ignoble to ponder on, repellent to discuss, illiberal to practice, infinite in number, trifling in their minuteness, and for all these reasons little likely to enhance the glory of the arts. Behind this opinion or mental disposition stands another exalted but deceitful view, from which it draws its force, to wit, the doctrine that truth is the native inhabitant of the human mind, not something that comes into it from outside, and that the senses do not inform the understanding but merely awaken it. Nor is this error or (to give it its true name) this alienation of the mind in the smallest degree corrected by those who have allowed to the senses their due place, that is to say, the first role. For these men, too, if we go by what they have actually done, have simply given up Natural History in the sense of a perambulation of the world. Instead they have based themselves in everything on the agitation of their own wit, content to circle round and round for ever amid the darkest idols of the mind under the high-sounding name of contemplation.

Bacon came to the conclusion that this quarrel with and divorce from particulars had thrown the human family into confusion.

1. A most important clue to the understanding of *De Sapientia Veterum*. Bacon sees in the fable he adduces an allegory of the begetting of false sciences like alchemy and magic (the Centaurs) by illegitimate violence (Ixion) on illusory material (a cloud in the likeness of Juno) in contrast to the reality (Nature and Art) begotten by the legitimate union of the true husband Jove with the real Juno. Cf. Sp. I, 573 (IV, 367); III, 503. Though he rejects this sort of interpretation of tradition, which was a fashion of the age, as a genuine method of scientific research, he was nevertheless soon to resort to it, as (a) not unworthy of investigation in itself and (b) a powerful means, if skilfully used, of creating the right attitude to a genuine science of nature.

(13. *Mistaken method of previous enquirers*)

A new subject of meditation: The resistance now offered to new knowledge is not the only obstacle. The human race might be so fortunate as to overcome these difficulties and break these chains. There is another point which demands the closest attention. What is the true character of the received philosophy, or of the various other philosophies, which, like planks from a wrecked ship, have been cast up on our shore? When he followed this path Bacon found that the Natural Philosophy we have received from the Greeks must rank only as the childhood of science. It has what is proper to boys. It is a great chatter-box and is too immature to breed.

Now of this philosophy Aristotle is by universal consent the chief, yet he left nature herself untouched and inviolate, and dissipated his energies in comparing, contrasting and analysing popular notions about her. How could anything solid be expected of a man who created a universe out of categories? What difference does it make whether one chooses as the first principles of things either Matter, Form and Privation or Substance, Quality and Relation? These are but words, and what is needed is to put something better in their place. It would be to forget oneself to proceed to a formal refutation of such a scheme, for there is no agreement about their first principles or the proper mode of demonstrating truth. On the other hand it would be both insolent and beneath the weight of the subject to turn the weapon of ridicule against a man who has won such authority as to be virtually the dictator of philosophy. But there can be no dispute that by his Logic (very naturally, indeed, since, as he liked to boast, he invented it all himself) he corrupted the philosophy of nature.

Leaving him we turn to Plato, a man without doubt of deeper understanding, who embraced the knowledge of Forms and made use of Induction,[1] not only for his first principles but throughout. Yet he failed in both. He sought only loose inductions and abstract forms and rested content therewith. On a closer consideration of the writings and the character of the man, he turns out to be not seriously interested in Natural Philosophy. Rather he seems to have taken it up only to preserve for himself the glorious title of philosopher and thus add an appearance of majesty to his moral and political teaching. He corrupted man's view of nature as much by his Theology as Aristotle did by his Logic. If the truth be spoken, he is as near to a poet as Aristotle is to a sophist.

1. Induction in Bacon means the *interpretation of nature* as opposed to the *anticipation of nature*; it is not strictly opposed to deduction.

(Importance of the Presocratics)

With these two we have the advantage that their opinions can be drawn from their original source, since their works are extant. But with the rest, Pythagoras, Empedocles, Heraclitus, Anaxagoras, Democritus, Parmenides, Xenophanes and others, the case is different. Their views are accessible to us only at second-hand, by report and in fragments. If, then, we are to make up for the injustice of their lot, this means a much greater effort of research as well as greater caution and deliberation in judging them. In pursuing any clue to information about them Bacon was scrupulously diligent. Aristotle confutes them, Cicero cites them, Plutarch made a small collection of their opinions, there are the *Lives* of Laertius and the poem of Lucretius, not to mention scattered references and mentions in other sources. All these Bacon read, candidly considered and judged. Of course it cannot be doubted that if their theories were extant in their own works they would present a greater strength and consistency; the force of a theory depends on a mutual fitness of the parts, one supporting another and each contributing to the proof of the whole. Handed down in fragments their views seem weak. Bacon allowed for this and formed no slight opinion of their worth. Amidst the variety of opinions not a few showed close observation of nature and careful assignment of causes; and, as was only to be expected, some succeeded better in some points, some in others. Exception should, perhaps, be made of Pythagoras. For, although his Numbers do contain some suggestion of Natural Philosophy, his discoveries and opinions were for the most part better suited to form the foundation of a religious order than a school of philosophy. This is borne out by the event. His teachings contributed more to the Manichaean heresy and the superstition of Mohammed than to natural philosophy.[1] The rest were certainly natural philosophers, some of whom penetrated into nature with more depth and insight than Aristotle did.

Aristotle, it must be confessed, busied himself, like an Ottoman Turk, in the slaughter of his brethren, and with success. Yet he cannot escape the judgment that must be passed on the Greeks as a whole. Their opinions and theories are like the arguments of so many stage-plays, devised to give an illusion of reality, with greater or less elegance, carelessness or frigidity. They have what is proper to a stage-play, a neat roundedness foreign to a

1. The reference is to the effect of Neoplatonism on Gnosticism, and, through it, on Manichaeism. The same tradition, ultimately deriving from Pythagoras, affected Arabian thinkers like Avicebron, whose *Fons Vitae* or *Fons Sapientiae* was much discussed by the Schoolmen from the middle of the twelfth century on.

narration of fact. Nor was it to be expected that the staging, or publication, of such theories could quickly end. What was there to check these aimless divagations of the human mind? Sect after sect would have continued to arise in Natural Philosophy, were it not that men's habits, tastes and political inclinations took a turn hostile to such novelties even in the speculative sphere. Here the analogy of Astronomy can help us. One party wants the earth to revolve, another wants to explain the apparent motions by eccentrics and epicycles, and what is visible in the heavens supports either opinion equally and gives no casting vote. Nay, even the calculations based on tables of observations suit either view. So it is with Natural Philosophy. Here, and with even greater facility, theories can be thought up, all different, all self-consistent, all pulling men's minds in different directions, and all appealing for support to the vulgar observations which in questions of this sort are allowed the role of judge.

Have there been in our time or the preceding generation any lack of men to think up new systems of nature? I myself remember the appearance on the stage of Telesius (1508-88) to present a new play with a plausible plot which, however, did not convince many. Not so long ago Fracastor (1483-1553), with no pretensions to founding a new sect, used his freedom of judgment and enquiry with a pleasing candour. Cardan (1501-76), a man of lesser weight, did the like. Then our fellow-countryman, Gilbert, having displayed great steadiness and constancy of judgment in his painstaking investigation of the magnet and deployed a great retinue, nay, an army of experiments in support, promptly threatened the foundation of a new sect in Natural Philosophy. He should have been warned by the fate of Xenophanes, to whose opinion he inclined; for his name was turned to ridicule.[1] These men, then, and any others now or hereafter of the same sort, ought to be classed with the mass of ancient thinkers from whom they do not essentially differ. They are men who venture to make pronouncements on the basis of a restricted number of observations, who touch nature only with the tips of their fingers, and do not so mingle themselves into her being as to attain either contemplative truth or works of utility.

Bacon, in short, believed that as an outcome of all these philosophies, elaborated through all these cycles of time, not one single experiment could be adduced which was effective in raising or enriching the condition of mankind and could at the same time be truthfully put to the credit of such

---

1. Sp. II, p. 136, note 1. The name Xenophanes (revealer of new things) was in mockery changed to Xenomanes (mad about novelties).

speculations. On the contrary, Aristotle's fiction of four elements, though it is true he rather lent his authority to it than originated it, was snapped up by the physicians and drew after it similar groups, of four characters, four humours, four primary qualities. Like a malignant and baleful star this brought sterility on Medicine and on many of the Mechanical Arts. Men suffered themselves to rest content with these elegant artificialities and convenient shortcuts, and troubled no further. Meanwhile it was about philosophies of this poor quality that the stir and buzz of speculation and argument arose so vividly foreshadowed in the legend of Scylla. That lady had the face and countenance of a maiden, but her loins were girt about with yelping hounds. So these doctrines present at first view a charming face, but the rash wooer who should essay the generative parts in hope of offspring, is blessed only with shrill disputes and arguments. Let it be said, however, by way of caution, that our rejection of these theories is no reflection on the intelligence or industry of their authors. It touches only the theories themselves. For the cruel truth is that if a man once abandons the light of nature, then the more eminent he be in intellect and zeal, the deeper he plunges into the obscure tortuous caverns where fantasies and idols dwell, and the harder it is for him to get out.

It must not be inferred, either, from Bacon's rejection of the general theories of these philosophers, that he approves the particular theories and secondary causes usually offered and sought in their writings. These are no more to be trusted than the general theories. For they are dependent on the general theories and exhibit an equal lack of strictness of method in research. They appeal only to the familiar and the obvious, in which the human mind contentedly acquiesces, but make no effort to get beneath the surface of nature. They still remain subject to the universal defect, that is, they seize on experiments and effects already known and do no more than hold them together by a flimsy network of logic cut to the precise measure of the familiar facts. This does not amount to the demonstration of some causal relation or some natural process opening the way to effects and experiments as yet unknown.

Having traversed the world of the received philosophy Bacon, eager to miss no possible path, cast his eyes towards that region of cloud and darkness, the secret recesses of remote antiquity. He knew well that, if he chose to act with less than absolute sincerity, it would not be difficult to convince men that among the sages of antiquity, long before the Greeks, a Science of Nature had flourished, of much more potency than theirs and sunk in deeper oblivion. He knew well what solemnity it would add to new discoveries to connect them with remote antiquity in the same way as self-made men invest themselves from the dubious traditions of the genealogists with the glory of some ancient stock. But Bacon was resolved to rely on the evidence of facts and avoid any sort of imposture. He reserved the right to an opinion of his own about those distant ages, but thought it must not be allowed to influence the business in hand. Whether or not discoveries now made had been known to the ancients and the knowledge had been extinguished and rekindled with the changes of human fortune, is a matter of no moment, just as it matters not at all whether the New World is the old Atlantis or is now discovered for the first time. For truth must be sought from the light of nature, not recovered from the darkness of antiquity.[1]

(Alchemy)

It may occur to some reader that nothing is being said about the art or philosophy of the Alchemists, and he may interpret this silence as meaning that Bacon, out of respect for that art, is unwilling to include it among the unproductive philosophies, since, in fact, it has produced useful inventions not a few for the benefit of mankind. There is a story very fit to be applied to this art which will explain Bacon's attitude. An old man bequeathed to his sons a treasure of gold buried in some unknown spot in his vineyard. The sons set to digging the vineyard and found no gold but won a fine harvest as the fruit of their labours. So the Sons of Chemistry, searching for gold which may or may not be there, have by their bustle and stir been of no small profit and service to mankind. But their discoveries take their rise and bear their fruit on no higher intellectual plane than those of the Mechanical Arts. They depend on mere experience. Their philosophy, their speculative work, is not sound, and it is certainly less entertaining than what I have called the stage-plays of the philosophers. True, their Triad of First Principles[2] is not a useless discovery, for it has a certain affinity with things. Nevertheless these men, habituated to a few experiments in distillation, have reduced the whole of Natural Philosophy to separations and liberations to the neglect of true changes. As for the theoretical structure which serves as the basis of their whole philosophy, it would not be accepted by any competent observer. They hold that there are four matrices or elements of things in which

1. A passage of great interest for the understanding of *De Sapientia Veterum* and its place in Bacon's works.
2. Salt, Sulphur, Mercury.

specific seeds mature their young. These Births, they say, are quadriform to match the differences of each element, with the result that in sky, air, water, earth nothing exists which has not some conjugate or parallel in each of the other three. This imaginary ordering of nature no true natural philosopher would admit even into his dreams.

(Magic)

The harmonies which have found favour with the devotees of Natural Magic are of the same sort. It is by Sympathies and Antipathies that the Magicians explain everything. Led by these idle and supine assumptions they ascribe wonderful virtues and powers to things. But Bacon felt some indulgence even towards them. Among their many fancies they now and again produce a true effect. These effects are better fitted to excite wonder at their novelty than any fruit of true utility. But anything new may prove to have some use. At least it shakes some trifle out of nature's lap and enables us to *see* better if not yet to *do* anything.

The conclusion: Neither in the theories of the Greeks nor of the moderns, neither in the tradition of Alchemy nor of Natural Magic is there promise of a major improvement in the condition of mankind. These studies should either be consigned to oblivion or left to the zeal of common and ordinary minds. The true Sons of Science should turn their faces in another direction.

(14. *Bacon's meaning of Induction*)

Bacon thought too that the methods of demonstration needed to be looked into. Demonstrations are philosophy in the making; as they are good or bad so will perfect or imperfect doctrines result. On examination it appeared that the methods in use are neither full nor reliable. It is not the senses that should be impugned, as has been done by some. Mistakes of particular facts made by the senses do not materially affect the final outcome in the sciences, for such mistakes can be discounted by an intellect furnished with reliable information. It is the intellect by itself, resting on nature alone without the support of any artificial discipline, which must be unhesitatingly pronounced unequal to cope with the subtlety of things. It is neither so capacious as to be able to take in and classify the multifarious array of particulars requisite for its instruction, nor so scoured and clean as to admit the genuine native images of things without some colouring from the imagination. Speaking generally, the human mind is a mirror so uneven as to distort the rays which fall upon it by its angularities. It is not a smooth flat surface. Furthermore, every individual, in consequence of his education, interests, and constitution is attended by a delusive power, his own familiar demon, which mocks his mind and troubles it with various unsubstantial spectres. But herein lies no excuse for scepticism. For while, as everyone knows, no steadiness of hand or nice judgment of eye suffices to draw a straight line or a perfect circle, yet, let a man take but a ruler or compass, and the thing is done. In the mechanical arts too it is only for trifling tasks the naked hands suffice; yet with the appropriate instrument or tool these same hands can cope with anything, no matter how big or how small. Such an instrument is the art of demonstration, and this we must enquire into.

We come then to Aristotle's oracle, as we may call it, the Syllogism, and we propose to despatch it in a few words. In subjects which are based upon opinion, like ethics and politics, it is certainly of use. Here it serves as a sort of helping hand to the operations of the mind. But it is quite unsuited and inadequate to cope with the subtlety and obscurity of nature. A syllogism consists of propositions, a proposition of words, and words are the counters or symbols of notions or mental concepts. If then the notions themselves, which are the life of the words, are vague, ignorant, ill-defined (and this is true of the vast majority of notions concerning nature), down the whole edifice tumbles.

The syllogism being disposed of, what have we left? Induction. This is the one last refuge and support. On it are centred all hopes. This is the method which by slow and faithful toil gathers information from things and brings it to the understanding. But even of this method all that men know is the name. Its meaning and use have eluded them till now. Men have been at fault both in its application and in its form. Impatient of delay and looking on all sides for short cuts, in a hurry to establish fixed points round which, like poles, their disputations might revolve, they applied induction only to the basic principles of the sciences, naïvely trusting to fill up the middle terms by syllogistic derivations. So much for the application. As for the form, though they had determined it accurately in the case of the syllogism, their treatment of induction was cursory and careless and produced no more than a simple and even puerile form, a form which proceeds only by simple enumeration and yields only doubtful, not necessary, conclusions.

Such being the result of the meditation on methods of demonstration, can it be wondered at that Bacon found himself in disagreement with both the ancients and the moderns? A wine-drinker and a water-drinker, says the familiar jest, cannot hold the same opinions; and, while *they* drink an intel-

lectual beverage which either flows from a natural source or has been raised
with slight labour from some well, Bacon prefers a draught prepared from
innumerable grapes, grapes matured and plucked in due season from selected
clusters, crushed in the press, purged and clarified in the vat; a draught moreover which has been so treated as to qualify its powers of inebriating, since
he is resolved to owe nothing to the heady fumes of vain imaginings.

The conclusion: The philosophies we have discussed stand condemned
not only as barren of works but as resting on modes of demonstration found
weak and treacherous. They are not only out of contact with things, but
deserted and betrayed by the props they had provided for themselves.

(15. *The need for a Philosophy of Invention*)

But it is not only the methods of demonstration that are at fault. The
methods of discovery, or invention, if indeed there be any, are just as much
in need of examination. And here Bacon found evidence not so much of
wandering from the true path, but simply of solitude and emptiness. He was
indeed dumbfounded at it. To think that no man among men should ever
have had it in his heart or on his mind to direct the resources of human wit
and intellect towards the arts and sciences and to pave a path towards that
goal! To think that this whole endeavour should have been, should still be,
left to the obscurity of tradition, the dizzy round of argument, the eddies and
whirlpools of chance and mere experience! He felt driven to condone the
strange practice of the Egyptians. Like other ancient peoples they deified
their inventors; and if they set up images even of brute beasts in their
temples, well, they had the excuse that the irrational animals have discovered
almost as many of nature's operations as men have done. Men indeed have
failed to use their prerogative of reason to this end. However, we must not
neglect to look into such discoveries as are made.

We may consider first the simple artless mode of discovery habitual to
men. All this amounts to is that everyone who makes the attempt first seeks
out and peruses what others have said on the subject and then adds his own
quota of thought. But it is a baseless procedure either to entrust oneself to the
authority of others or to solicit, to invoke, one's own spirit to deliver oracles.
Next comes the kind of discovery or research in favour with the dialecticians.
It shares no more than the name with what we have in mind. The dialecticians are not concerned to seek out the principles and axioms on which arts
depend; they look only for logical consistency. When exceptionally keen
and persistent researchers come to bother them with their questions, the

dialecticians' practice is to urge them to put their trust in, nay, to take an oath of blind loyalty to, the existent art, such as it is. Finally, there are inventions due to experience pure and simple. If it just happens, it is called chance; if it has been sought after, it is called experiment. But these are only examples of what the proverb calls the broom that has come untied. Those who try to discover the nature or mode of operation of anything by the repetition of random experiments are never at one stay. They alternate between puzzled inaction or giddy activity; hot on the trail one moment, covered with confusion the next; their one discovery being the need for further investigation. How could it be otherwise? To imagine that the nature of anything can be found by examining that thing in isolation, is a notion born of ignorance and inexperience. The nature one seeks may be latent in some things, but manifest and palpable in others; in some things a matter for astonishment, in others too common to notice. There is, for example, a property in bodies which makes them hold together. Water-bubbles seem to shut themselves up in little hemispherical membranes; the force by which they do this strikes us as something mysterious and ingenious. The force which holds wood or stone together we take for granted, and give them the name of solid.

Bacon's conclusion was that men should perhaps be called rather unlucky than ignorant. It is not that they have not exerted themselves; but ill-luck or fond illusions have deflected them from their course.

(16. *The time has come for a fresh start*)

It is time an end were put to this desperation, or at least to these laments. We must decide once for all whether it would be better to abandon the endeavour and rest content with what we have, or make a serious exertion to improve our lot. The first step to this end is to set up in view the worthiness and excellence of the aim proposed, and so kindle greater enthusiasm for hard work on an exacting business. In this connection Bacon recalled how in antiquity extravagant enthusiasm led men to accord divine honours to inventors; while on those who deserved well of their fellows in civil affairs, on founders of cities and empires, Lawmakers, Liberators of their country from long-standing evils, over-throwers of tyrants, and others of this ilk, the style of Heroes only was conferred. Not for nothing, Bacon reflected, was this distinction observed in ancient times; for the benefits inventors confer extend to the whole human race, while those of civil heroes are confined to particular regions and narrower circles of human settlement. And there is this too. Inventions come without force or disturbance to bless the life of mankind, while civil changes rarely proceed without uproar and violence. If then the utility of some one particular invention so impresses men that they exalt to superhuman rank the man who is responsible for it, how much more noble would that discovery be which should contain within itself the potentiality of all particular inventions, and open up to the human spirit a path of direct and easy access to new remoter powers. Take an example from history. In olden days, when men directed their course at sea by observation of the stars, they merely skirted the shores of the old continent or ventured to traverse small land-locked seas. They had to await the discovery of a more reliable guide, the needle, before they crossed the ocean and opened up the regions of the New World. Similarly, men's discoveries in the arts and sciences up till now are such as could be made by intuition, experience, observation, thought; they concerned only things accessible to the senses. But, before men can voyage to remote and hidden regions of nature, they must first be provided with some better use and management of the human mind. Such a discovery would, without a doubt, be the noblest, the truly masculine birth of time.

Again Bacon noted that, in the Scriptures, King Solomon, though blessed with empire, gold, splendour of architecture, satellites, servants, ministers and slaves of every kind and degree, with a fleet to boot, and a glorious name and with the flattering admiration of the world, yet prided himself on none of these things. Instead he declared that *It was the glory of God to conceal a thing, the glory of a King to find it out*; as if the divine nature enjoyed the kindly innocence of such hide-and-seek, hiding only in order to be found, and with characteristic indulgence desired the human mind to join Him in this sport. And indeed it is this glory of discovery that is the true ornament of mankind. In contrast with civil business it never harmed any man, never burdened a conscience with remorse. Its blessing and reward is without ruin, wrong or wretchedness to any. For light is in itself pure and innocent; it may be wrongly used, but cannot in its nature be defiled.

Bacon next considered the nature of human ambition and found it to be of three kinds, one perhaps not worthy of the name. The first is of those men who with restless striving seek to augment their personal power in their own country. This is the vulgar and degenerate sort. The second is of those who seek to advance the position of their own country in the world; and this may be allowed to have more worth in it and less selfishness. The third is of those whose endeavour is to restore and exalt the power and dominion of man himself, of the human race, over the universe. Surely this is nobler and holier than the former two. Now the dominion of man over nature rests only on knowledge. His power of action is limited to what he knows. No force avails to break the chain of natural causation. Nature cannot be conquered but by obeying her.

This put Bacon upon thinking of examples to illustrate not simply the force of inventions but how such force is accompanied by rewards and blessings. This force is most plainly seen in those three inventions unknown to antiquity, and whose origins are still to us obscure and inglorious, to wit, Printing, Gunpowder and the Nautical Needle. These three, few in number, and not lying much out of the way, have changed the face and status of the world of men, first in learning, next in warfare, and finally in navigation. On them have followed countless changes, as a close scrutiny reveals. In fact, no empire, no school, no star seems to have exerted a greater influence on human affairs than these mechanical inventions. As for their value, the soonest way to grasp it is this. Consider the abyss which separates the life of men in some highly civilised region of Europe from that of some savage, barbarous tract of New India. So great is it that the one man might appear a god to the other, not only in respect of any service rendered but on a comparison of their ways of life. And this is the effect not of soil, not of climate, not of physique, but of the arts. Thus, in the geographical world, the old is much more civilised than the new. In the scientific world this is not so. On the contrary, recent acquisitions must be held the more important. They do not, like the old, merely exert a gentle guidance over nature's course; they have the power to conquer and subdue her, to shake her to her foundations. For the rule is that what discoveries lie on the surface exert but little force. The roots of things, where strength resides, are buried deep.

It may be that there are some on whose ear my frequent and honourable mention of practical activities makes a harsh and unpleasing sound because they are wholly given over in love and reverence to contemplation. Let them bethink themselves that they are the enemies of their own desires. For in nature practical results are not only the means to improve well-being but the guarantee of truth. The rule of religion, that a man should show his faith by his works, holds good in natural philosophy too. Science also must be known by works. It is by the witness of works, rather than by logic or even observation, that truth is revealed and established. Whence it follows that the improvement of man's mind and the improvement of his lot are one and the same thing.

Bacon drew the conclusion that all he has said about the worthiness of the end which he has marked out and measured in his mind is not exaggerated but falls short of the truth.

(17. *Omens favourable to Research*)

But, since what has been said about the excellence of the end may be regarded as a dream, let us consider with full care what hopeful prospect there is and in what quarter it shows itself. We must not suffer ourselves to become prisoners of a vision of supreme goodness and beauty and so abandon, or impair, the strictness of our judgment. Rather we should apply the rule current in civil affairs and be suspicious on principle and look on the dark side of human prospects. Let us cast aside all slighter hopes and vigorously canvass even those that seem most firm. In this determination Bacon consulted the auspices with all due care; and here the first thing that struck him was that the business in hand, being eminently good, was manifestly of God, and in the works of His hand small beginnings draw after them great ends. Then the omens from the nature of Time were also good. All concur that truth is the daughter of Time. How pusillanimous, then, to grovel before authors but to allow to Time, the author of authors and of all authority, less than his due! Nor were his hopes drawn only from the universal character of time, but from the special prerogative of our own age. The opinion men cherish about Antiquity is ill-considered and ill-suited to the word. The term should mean the ripe age, the fullness of years, of the whole world. Now among men we expect greater knowledge of affairs and more maturity of judgment from an old man in proportion to his experience and the multitude of things he has seen, heard and pondered; so from our modern age, if it but realised its powers and would put them boldly to the trial, far greater things are to be expected than from those distant days; for the world has grown older and immeasurably increased its store of experience and observation. It ought not to go for nothing that through the long voyages and travels which are the mark of our age many things in nature have been revealed which might throw new light on natural philosophy. Nay, it would be a disgrace for mankind if the expanse of the material globe, the lands, the seas, the stars, was opened up and brought to light, while, in contrast with this enormous expansion, the bounds of the intellectual globe should be restricted to what was known to the ancients.

It is worth bearing in mind, too, that the political conditions of Europe in this age are favourable. England is stronger, France is restored to peace, Spain is exhausted, Italy and Germany are undisturbed. The balance of power is restored and, in this tranquil state of the most famous nations, there is a turning towards peace; and peace is fair weather for the sciences to flourish.[1] Nor is the state of letters unfavourable. Rather, it has many auspicious aspects. By the Art of Printing, a thing unknown to antiquity, the discoveries and thoughts of individuals are now spread abroad like a flash of lightning. Religious controversies have become a weariness of the spirit, and men are perhaps more ready to contemplate the power, wisdom, and goodness of God in His works. Still, let us assume we have to do with a man who is overwhelmed by the unanimity and duration of the world's acquiescence in the opinions of former days. If such a man considers closely he cannot fail to see that leaders of opinion are but few and that all the rest, their followers, are but ciphers. They have never given a valid assent to the general opinion, for this results from an act of independent judgment. All they have managed to do is to make the step from ignorance to prejudice. If, then, the unanimity of these opinions is an illusion, so is their duration. On examination it shrinks to very narrow bounds. Suppose we allow twenty-five centuries to the recorded history of mankind. Of these scarce five can be set apart as propitious towards, and fruitful in, scientific progress, and the kind of sciences they cultivated were as far as possible removed from that natural philosophy we have in mind. Three periods only can be counted when the wheel of knowledge really turned: one among the Greeks, the second with the Romans, the last among the nations of Western Europe. All other ages have been given over to wars or other pursuits. So far as any scientific harvest is concerned they were barren wastes.

Another favourable omen is found in an understanding of the power and true nature of Chance. Chance, operating in suitable circumstances, has prompted many discoveries. This explains why, in the discovery of fire, the Prometheus of New India followed a different course from the European Prometheus. Flint is scarce in New India. Clearly in inventions which depend on the availability of suitable materials chance plays a large part; in inventions remote from daily experience, a smaller one; yet, be its role big or little, in every age it is the fertile parent of discoveries, nor have we any reason to suppose it has grown old and past bearing. Bacon accordingly opined that, since discoveries occur even when men are not looking for them and are thinking of something else, it is reasonable to expect that when men *are*

1. Bacon's optimism here is facile. The Thirty Years War and the English Revolution were at hand.

looking for them, and that not in fits and starts but systematically and methodically, many more discoveries will be made. Of course it happens now and again that a man stumbles by accident on what has eluded the earnest search of another; but the opposite is the normal thing. The action of chance is intermittent, undesigned, random; art acts steadily, purposively, co-operatively.

A happy omen for the discovery of what still lies hid may be drawn also from what has already been brought to light. For many discoveries are of such a kind that, before they were made, nobody could have entertained the least notion of them. Men's anticipations of the new are fashioned on the model of the old. The old governs their imagination. Yet this is a completely fallacious pattern of thought. There is no universal law that discoveries fetched up from the source and fount of things must flow down to us along familiar channels. Suppose, before the invention of cannon, somebody had described, not the thing, but its effect. Suppose him to have said: An invention has been made by which walls and fortifications of the greatest strength are battered and levelled from a great distance. Would not his hearers have indulged in all sorts of speculations about the multiplication by weights and wheels and so forth of the power of artillery relying on torsion? Would the idea of a violent explosion have entered anyone's imagination? They would have seen no example of such a thing save an earthquake or thunderbolt, already rejected by them as incapable of imitation. Or suppose, before the discovery of silk, somebody had remarked: There exists a kind of thread useful for clothes and furnishings which is far finer than cotton or wool and at the same time stronger, handsomer, softer. Men would have begun to think of some vegetable silk, or superfine animal hair, or of the feathers or down of birds. But who would have thought of a worm spinning, and spinning so copiously, and year after year? Indeed, if anyone had let fall the word 'worm', he would have been a target for mirth with his dreams about this new kind of spider's web. These examples should help us to think about the secrets still locked in Nature's bosom. They are such as to elude and mock the imagination and thought of men. So, Bacon reflected, if a man puts the rein on his hopes of fresh discoveries because, on the evidence of what he sees about him, he regards them as impossible or improbable, he needs to be admonished that he does not know enough even to frame an intelligent and reasonable wish.

But another train of thought led Bacon in the opposite direction, some of the discoveries already made being of a very different, almost directly opposite, kind to those last spoken of. For they give confidence that there may well be splendid discoveries lying at our feet which we pass unnoticed. It is probably true that the discovery of gunpowder, silk, the mariner's compass, sugar, glass, rest on the hidden properties of things; but printing involved nothing more than the combination of things already known, things that lay on the surface, as one might say. In truth, in this business of discovery, the human mind is so clumsy, so inept, that it first despairs of the impossible and then despises itself for missing the obvious. First it thinks it incredible that such and such a discovery should be made, then incredible that it was not made long ago. This gives ground for hope that a vast number of inventions depend, not on the ferreting out of mysterious operations, but on the transference and application of processes already known.

Good and cheerful auspices were also drawn by Bacon from the Mechanical Arts, when he considered their progress, especially in comparison with philosophy. By their daily ripening to perfection they seem to reveal the possession of some vital breath, while philosophy, like a statue, is surrounded by crowds of worshippers but never moves. With their first originators the Mechanical Arts show themselves rude, uncouth, unwieldy; but later they gain in strength and grace. Philosophy begins at the height of its vigour with the founder of each school, and subsequently declines. Nor is there any better explanation of these opposite destinies than that, in Mechanics, the wits of many men combine to serve one end, in Philosophy one authority destroys the wits of others. For as soon as men surrender to authority they cease to be creative and take their servile station as bodyguards of one man. Thus philosophy, torn away from its roots in experience, whence it derived its first vigorous shoot and growth, droops and dies.

Apprised by this thought Bacon noted also another fact. In both the arts and sciences there is a universally accepted cleavage into the Empirical and the Rational or Philosophical. But in Bacon's view these twin attitudes have not up to now been properly mingled and combined. The Empirics are like ants; they gather and consume. The Rationalists are spiders spinning webs out of themselves. But the bee combines both functions. It gathers its material from flowers of garden and field, and digests and transforms them by a faculty of its own. This is the type of true philosophy. It takes the matter furnished by natural history and mechanical experience and stores it in its memory, but not before it has been transformed and wrought upon by the understanding. Bacon is, of course, aware that some Empirics disclaim the title of Empiric pure and simple, and some Dogmatists are ambitious to be thought determined and intelligent experimentalists. But, whichever group they belong to, these pretensions are only evidence of their wish to have a reputation above their fellows. In fact the divorce between the two activities, speculation and experiment, has always obtained. But if the two could be joined in a closer and holier union the prospects of a numerous and happy issue are bright indeed.

There is also this further ground for comfort. When he reviewed the infinite expenditure of brains, time, and money on objects and pursuits which, fairly judged, are useless, Bacon was certain that a small portion of this expenditure devoted to sane and solid purposes could triumph over every obstacle. Men shrink back from the multiplicity of particular facts. Yet the phenomena of the arts are easily grasped in comparison with the fictions of the mind once they break free from the control of factual evidence. Thus all the arguments adduced above urge us on to adopt a hopeful view. But the surest ground of hope is in the mistakes of the past. When the affairs of a commonwealth had been mismanaged, there was comfort in the remark: The blacker the past, the brighter the hope for the future. In philosophy, too, if the old errors are abandoned (and to be made aware of them is the first step to amendment), things will take a turn for the better. But if men had been on the right path all those ages past and yet had got no further, what hope could there be? Then it would have been clear that the difficulty lay in the material to be investigated (which is out of our contol), not in the instrument, that is to say, the human mind and its management, which is ours to improve. As things are, it is plain that there are no insuperable or immovable objects in the way; simply it lies in a direction untrodden by the feet of men. It may frighten us a little by its loneliness; it offers no other threat. A new world beckons. Even if the breezes that reach us from it were of far less promise and hope, Bacon was resolved that the trial should be made. Not to try is a greater hazard than to fail. If we fail, it is the loss but of a trifling effort. Not to try is to forgo the prospect of measureless good.

The conclusion of this meditation, of what has been said and left unsaid, is that there is no lack of hope. There is hope enough both to launch the man of enterprise on the venture and to convince the deep and sober mind of the likelihood of success.

(18. *General considerations of procedure*)

Zeal being kindled and hope raised, Bacon's next thought was of the mode of accomplishing his end. These, then, are the steps he suggests, couched, as seemed fit, in candid, unvarnished terms. First, since something quite new is to be put in hand, the safest oracle for the future lies in the rejection of the past. Current theories, opinions, notions, should be brushed aside, so far as a disciplined firmness of mind may be able to achieve it; and the understanding must be brought into contact with facts in a straightforward unprejudiced way. One might say that the kingdom of nature is like the kingdom of heaven, to be approached only by becoming like a little child. A great storehouse of facts should be accumulated, both from natural history and from the experience of the mechanical arts. It should be sufficient in quantity, diversity, reliability, and subtlety, to inform the mind; and of the two sources of information the greater reliance should be placed in the mechanical arts, because nature betrays her secrets more fully when in the grip and under the pressure of art than when in enjoyment of her natural liberty.

Further, the material collected should be sorted into orderly Tables, so that the understanding may work upon it and thus accomplish its appropriate task. After the particulars have been arranged in Tables, there should be no immediate hurry to press on with the collection of new facts, although collecting facts is a useful thing and is the equivalent of what might be called 'literate experience.'[1] For the time has now come to ascend to generalisations. The understanding is endowed by nature with an evil impulse to jump from particulars to the highest axioms (what are called First Principles). This impulse must be held in check; but generalisations lying close to the facts may first be made, then generalisations of a middle sort, and progress thus achieved up the successive rungs of a genuine ladder of the intellect.

Bacon accordingly thought that a new form of Induction must be devised. This kind of Induction must accept the proviso that conclusions drawn from a limited number of facts would be valid only on proof that no contradictory instance[2] could be found. He sought to avoid the risk of pronouncing on the basis of too few instances superficially selected. For that, as one of the ancients said, is to look for knowledge in one's private world, not in the public world of men. A valid axiom, in his view, should not be narrowly cut to the measure of the facts from which it is drawn. It should have a more ample scope, permitting the inclusion of new facts under it by which its final limits would

1. For the important conception of ' literate experience' see note 2, p. 119.
2. The word 'instance' needs a definition. It is more than a mere phenomenon of nature. It is an observed fact that has entered into and formed part of a logical structure, or in his own words, been 'transformed and wrought upon by the understanding'.

be fixed. He looked also for other discoveries not aimed so much at the per-
fecting of his design as at speeding up its application and producing a prompt
harvest for mankind. For the soundness or otherwise of all these proposals he
was prepared, if necessary, to appeal against the judgment of opinion and
stand by the verdict of results.[1]

(19. *Scope of the work. Proposed tables of data*)

He thought, also, that the business in hand is not an opinion to be held but
a work to be done. Its aim is to lay the foundation, not of any school or view,
but of boundless riches and wellbeing. This creates an obligation not only to
get the work done, but to share it and pass it on. These are matters of equal
concern. But Bacon could not fail to observe that men, in respect of the
knowledge they think they have, resolve the problem of publication or con-
cealment with nothing in mind but their own reputation and renown. So it
comes about that men with the least valuable wares offer them in a dim
deceptive light as the safest path to their own glory. Bacon, however, thought
he had in hand a matter too noble to be sullied by ambition or pretence.
Nevertheless, not being quite a novice in the ways of the world or the move-
ments of men's minds, he thought fit to make some preparations for the road.
He could not forget that inveterate prejudices, like the delusions of the insane,
must be artfully circumvented rather than exasperated by violent opposition.
Accordingly, to avoid fanning rather than quenching the flames of contention, and with due regard to simplicity and candour, he recognised the
desirability of a certain measure of prudent conformity. To this end he
proposed a work on the interpretation of nature and on nature itself, designed
to eradicate errors with the least possible offence and thus to effect a peaceable
entry into the apprehensions of men. This, he thought, should be all the
easier, as he did not propose to put himself forward as leader or guide, but to
elicit and spread light from nature herself, thus precluding for the future the
need of a leader.

Meanwhile time was passing; he was himself immersed beyond his wish in
civil business; and when he thought on the uncertainty of life, delay became
unbearable. He felt the need to secure at least some part of his plan, and
decided to put forward a simpler statement, which, though not published,
might yet suffice to prevent the miscarriage of a thing so wholesome. So,
after long and anxious thought, he decided that the first thing necessary was

---

1. These last sentences touch on the point of Bacon's willingness to take over the direction
of a research institute and test the validity of his views.

to set forth Tables of Discovery, or, as it were, formulae of a legitimate mode of research, in certain fields, to serve as an example and to be a sort of visible embodiment of the work to be done.[1] This seemed the best way to distinguish the true from the false path; to put it beyond doubt that what is proposed is as far as possible from being a matter of mere words; and so to frighten off, on the one hand, the man who has no confidence in the project, and, on the other, anyone who seeks to magnify it unduly. No doubt, when the tables are produced, a certain doubt, or despair, of completing similar tables for other branches of research will depress the feebler spirits; and they will qualify their approval of the pattern by bewailing the absence of further rules and directions. But many more will be stimulated to make the utmost use of the tables and to look for the final key of interpretation. Even by such a key as is now provided their zeal will be kindled to catch a glimpse of a new aspect of nature.

For himself Bacon was minded not to yield to his own or to anyone's impatience, but to keep his eyes fixed on the ultimate success of the project. He would therefore communicate his tables only to a few and keep the rest back till after the publication of a treatise for popular perusal. Looking ahead he could see that the stronger and loftier minds, advised by what he now had to offer and without waiting for greater aids, would not only aspire but succeed in achieving the rest for themselves. Briefly his view was that it was true, as someone remarked, that men of sense would find enough here to meet their needs and fools would not be helped by more. But he did not intend to slacken his own efforts. Without some introduction the tables could not serve as a starting point for teaching. They needed a preface, and this he hopes the present writing might supply, for that was the intention of every word in it.

This further he would have known. He has no pretensions, like other teachers in the arts, of insisting on the use of any particular formula of research. All he would claim is, that after trying everything, he came, as the result of long experience and (he thinks) some power of judgment, to the formula which he has approved and offers to others as the most reliable and useful. Others may enjoy greater leisure, or they may profit by being freed of the difficulties that beset the pioneers, or they may be endowed with a deeper and more capacious understanding. They will carry on the work and Bacon has no wish to block their path. Quite the contrary. His declared opinion is that the art of discovery must itself improve with the progress of

1. Sp. III, 625.

The Refutation of Philosophies

Introductory Narrative

I am preparing a refutation of philosophies but know not how to begin. The road which lies open for others is closed to me. The hosts of errors are so many and so great that it is impossible to engage them singly. They must be overthrown and swept away in masses. To engage with them one by one in single combat would be pointless. To justify such a debate there must be agreement about first principles. But that is lacking. What is more, I reject the forms and deny the validity of their proofs and demonstrations. As a last resource I might try to establish my positions on the basis of sense evidence and experience. But, if I do this, we are back where we began. I have made a special point about the necessity of a preliminary preparation of the mind. I must not forget this and start off in the opposite direction. I must not attempt a direct, abrupt encounter with things themselves, for they need to be approached by opening up and levelling a special path on account of the inveterate prejudices and obsessions of our minds. To ignore this would be to betray myself. Therefore I must devise an approach in keeping with my purpose. First I shall adduce certain 'signs' which will put us in a position to pass judgment on philosophies. Then, with a view to undermining their authority, I shall point out, within the philosophies themselves, certain monstrous errors and intellectual absurdities.

It does not escape me that the metal of these errors is too firmly set to yield to satire. That kind of boastful confidence which rejects opinions without being able to confute them is only too familiar to the learned. I intend no criticism too slight or too base for the majesty of the question at issue. I do not want the support that might be won by a refutation of this sort. I appeal only to the patience and fairness of lofty and resolute minds. A man may earnestly wish to rescue himself from long association with error; the motives which prompt him to join my cause may be generous and noble; but he still needs to know what he ought to think about the ancient and received opinions. It remains true, however, that the human mind is not like a wax tablet. On a tablet you cannot write the new till you rub out the old; on the mind you cannot rub out the old except by writing in the new.

This is the demand that must be met. Our course, to speak plainly, must be to attract the willing, not to force the reluctant. As implied at the outset, we abjure all violence. A witty saying of Borgia about the expedition of Charles VIII into Italy is *à propos*. The French, he said, came with chalk in their hands to mark off their billets, not with arms to force an entry. We intend a similar course of action and anticipate a similar success. We seek a peaceful lodging in able and congenial minds, not a scuffle with those of contrary views.

But, as things have fallen out, in that part of our project on which we are now engaged, that is, the refutation of philosophies, a surprising piece of good luck has come to our aid. While I was immersed in the business a friend came to see me who had just returned from France. When we had exchanged greetings and personal news, 'Tell me', said he, 'what are you writing in the intervals of public business, or at least when public business is less pressing?' 'Your enquiry is timely', said I, 'for, just in case you think I have nothing on hand, I am planning an Instauration of Philosophy, containing nothing empty or abstract, but designed to improve the conditions of human life.' 'A noble task', said he. 'Who is helping you?' 'You must understand', I replied, 'that I am working in complete isolation.' 'That is a hard lot', said he, and immediately added, 'But take it from me that there are others who have the matter at heart.' Filled with joy I exclaimed, 'You have restored me to life. I had come to believe my child would perish in the wilderness.' 'Well', said he, 'would you like me to tell you what happened to me in France?' 'I'ld like nothing better', said I, 'and you shall have my thanks to boot.'

Then he told me that in Paris a friend had taken him along and introduced him to a gathering, 'the sight of which', he said, 'would rejoice your eyes. It was the happiest experience of my life.' There were some fifty men there, all of mature years, not a young man among them, all bearing the stamp of dignity and probity. He picked out among them officers of state, senators, distinguished churchmen, people from all ranks of life, and foreigners from various nations. At his entry they were chatting easily among themselves but sitting in rows as if expecting somebody. Not long after there entered to them a man of peaceful and serene air, save that his face had become habituated to the expression of pity. They all stood up in his honour, and he looked round and said with a smile: 'It is more than I can understand, as recognise you one by one, how you can all be at leisure at the same time. Iow is it to be explained?' Then one of the company replied, 'You yourself are the explanation, for we all put what you have to tell us above any other business.' 'Then', said he, 'I am incurring a heavy responsibility for the total of time that will be lost here, during which you might all be going about your several tasks serving I know not how many men. I must not keep you waiting any longer.' Which said, he took his seat, not on a platform or pulpit, but on level with the rest and delivered the following address. My friend gave me a record of it which he made at the time. It was the best he could do, but he had to admit that when he went over it at home with the friend who had introduced him they found it very inferior to the original.

The Address

We are agreed, my sons, that you are men. That means, as I think, that you are not animals on their hind legs, but mortal gods. God, the creator of the universe and of you, gave you souls capable of understanding the world but not to be satisfied with it alone. He reserved for himself your faith, but gave the world over to your senses. Neither of these oracles did he wish to be clear, but wrapped in obscurity. Yet have you no ground for complaint that he makes you exert yourselves. Your reward is to know the excellence of things. Now, so far as the things of God are concerned, I have the best hopes for you; but as regards human things I fear you are wrapped in eternal night. If I am not mistaken you are convinced that the state of your sciences is sound and flourishing. For my part I warn you not to over-estimate the abundance or utility of what you have. It does not mark the pinnacle of your attainment, it does not give you mastery of your desires, it does not mean the end of your task.

Look at it this way. The vast variety of our scientific writings makes up a huge and luxuriant growth. But interrogate and cross-question those writings on their real content. Everywhere you will find endless repetition of the same thing. The words, the ordering, the examples, the illustrations may vary. But the sum total, the weight, the real power, amounts to a mere sample or token repeated over and over again. The splendour turns out to be penury. You have managed to get a sensation of fullness on Lenten fare. If I may divert you with a homely illustration, your learning is like the banquet of the Chalcidian host. When his guests asked where he had found such a variety of game, he replied: 'The variety is only in the sauces, the meat is a pig from my own back-yard.'

You would not, I think, seek to deny that the whole of our great learning is merely a surviving fragment of Greek philosophy. Nor was this creature bred and nurtured in the glades and thickets, but in schools and cells, like a domestic animal being fattened. Suppose we leave aside the Greeks (and they are only a handful), what have the Romans, or Arabs, or our own age to offer, that is not drawn from the discoveries of Aristotle, Plato, Hippocrates, Galen, Euclid, and Ptolemy, or is reducible to them? Your riches are but the personal properties of these few men. Your hopes and your fortunes are precariously concentrated in the brains of these six. God did not give you rational souls in order that you should place in men the faith you owe to Him. He did not give you reliable and trustworthy senses in order that you might study the writings of a few men. Study the Heaven and the Earth, the works of God himself, and do so while celebrating His praises and singing hymns to your Creator. The six, of course, can join the choir too, if wanted. There's room for all.

Your doctrine, originating in Greece and adopted by you, which steps forward with such pride and show, was it not only a fragment of the whole of Greek wisdom? Greek wisdom was manifold; and though variety may not accord with truth, at least it prevents error becoming fixed. Variety is as the rainbow to the sun. Of all images the rainbow is the most evanescent and fleeting, yet it is an image. But this Greek variety was extinguished for us by Aristotle, himself a Greek. Perhaps he wished to rival the exploits of his pupil Alexander,

> That prosperous brigand of a global size
> Who set the evil dream before men's eyes
> That one man might all lands engross.[1]

Or was the master not a prosperous brigand of learning? Perhaps that is too severe; yet the rest of the passage fits like a glove. By no means can he who reduced so many splendid intellects, so many free minds, to mental slavery be called a benefactor of the human-race.

My sons, you have learned how restricted your abundance is; how it reduces itself to a handful of thinkers. Next, pray, consider its usefulness. But how am I to find a way to your understanding and your senses? I do not anticipate a refusal, for you are kind. But it is a question of engineering a new path, no easy task. There is in you a native spark of reason which I would blow upon and excite, if I could rescue you from the dazzle of an alien and intrusive beam. How can I give myself to you in such a way as to restore you to yourselves? Infinite are the prejudices that have sprung up, the false opinions that have been adopted, given lodging, passed on to others. The theologians, for instance, have borrowed freely from that philosophy and have thus established a system of speculation in which the doctrines of both are combined. Men engaged in affairs of state, thinking it helpful to their standing to pass for learned, liberally besprinkle their writings and their speeches with wisdom from the same spring. Sayings and

---

1. Lucan, *Pharsalia* x, 20–8, a description of the visit of Julius Caesar to the tomb of Alexander the Great. Bacon extracts from the passage, with a little violence to the order of the words but no alteration of the sense, a condemnation of world-dominion. Perhaps, as usual, he quoted from memory.

terms have been coined under the influence of that same philosophy and in agreement with its dictates and decrees. Nay, from the moment you learn to speak you are under the necessity of drinking in and assimilating what perhaps I may be allowed to call a hotch-potch of errors. Nor do these errors derive their strength only from popular usage. They are sanctioned by the institutions of academies, colleges, orders, and even states themselves. Can all this be renounced in a moment? Is this what I ask you to do?

My sons, that is not what I ask. I have no objection to your enjoying the fruits of your philosophy. I do not disallow them. I do not wish to hurry you into isolation. Use your philosophy; let your arguments be nourished at her breast; adorn your conversation with its jewels; profess it in public and increase your gravity thereby in the eyes of the masses. The new philosophy will bring you no such gains. It does not lie upon the surface. It cannot be gathered in passing. It does not flatter the mind by fitting in with its pre-conceptions. It does not sink to the capacity of the vulgar except in so far as it benefits them by its works. Therefore keep your old philosophy. Use it when convenient. Keep one to deal with nature and the other to deal with the populace. Every man of superior understanding in contact with inferiors wears a mask.[1] If I may, as my habit is, speak freely among friends, then I advise you: Possess Lais but do not let her possess you.[2] Hold firm to your own judgment. Give yourself to others, but not completely. Keep yourselves for better things. Am I right that you feel my requirements less of a burden, since I suffer you to retain in use and honour the philosophy you already have? But will you not, in return for that concession, allow me to call in question its utility and truth?

But suppose you were minded to give up all you have been taught and have believed; suppose, in return for an assurance of the truth of my view, you were prepared to abandon your favourite views and arguments; I should still be at a loss, for I do not know how to convince you of a thing so novel and unexpected. The difficulty is that the usual rules of argument do not apply since we are not agreed on first principles. Even the hope of a basis of discussion is precluded, since I cast doubt on the forms of proof now in use and mean to attack them. In the present mental climate I cannot safely entrust the truth to you. Your understandings must be prepared before they

1. The Latin here is: *Nemo enim est qui plus multo quam alius quis intelligit, quin ad minus intelligentem tamquam personatus sit, ut se exuat, alteri det.* Not being able to extract a satisfactory sense from the last five words I have omitted them.

2. The philosopher Aristippus, being reproved for consorting with the famous courtesan. Lais, replied: 'I possess Lais, not she me.' Diogenes Laertius, *Lives of the Philosophers* II, 74–5.

can be instructed; your minds need healing before they can be exercised; the site must be cleared before it can be built upon; and this is the sole purpose of our being here today. Is there, then, any procedure by which we can have a profitable discussion? We must not give up hope. Undoubtedly, sons, there is in the human soul some portion of our understanding, however preoccupied and beset, which welcomes truth, and there is a path which leads down thereto by a gentle incline.

Come, then, my sons. Let us on both sides put off any pretensions we may have to learning. Let us assume the character of simple folk. Let us not discuss the essence of things but try to draw some tentative conclusions from external 'signs'. In this at least we shall be acting like common men.

Your learning, we have said, is derived from the Greeks. But what sort of people were they? I mean to go in for no abuse. I shall neither repeat nor imitate what others have said. I am content simply to remark that that nation was always precipitate mentally and professorial by habit – two characteristics inimical to wisdom and truth. We must not shut our ears to the words of the Egyptian priest, spoken to a distinguished Greek statesman and recorded by a famous Greek author.[1] For he spoke like a true oracle when he said: 'You Greeks are always children.' Children they were, not only in their knowledge of the past but even more in their natural philosophy. What could be more childlike than a philosophy prompt to chatter and argue and incapable of begetting works, a philosophy inept in dispute and empty of results? Let me remind you, in the words of the prophet,[2] of the rock from which ye were hewn and bid you reflect that the nation whose authority you follow is the Greek.

So much for the first 'sign'. Now for the second, to wit, the character of the age in which philosophy was born and launched on its career. It took its rise, sons, in an age that bordered on fables, was poor in historical knowledge, was little informed or enlightened by travel and knowledge of the earth, lacked both the respect for antiquity and the wealth of our modern times, and was deficient in dignity and precedent. We are free indeed, to believe that there were divine heroes in ancient times with wisdom loftier than the common condition of mankind. But it must be conceded that our age, even making no claims for the labours of great minds and the fruit of their meditations, enjoys in comparison with the past the experience of some two thousand years of history and the knowledge of two-thirds of the surface of the globe.

1. Spoken to Solon, reported by Plato.   2. Isaiah 51, 1.

Whether, then, you reckon times or spaces, you see within what narrow confines the great intellects of those ages moved, or were shut in. A history worthy of the name did not extend over a thousand years. The rest was but legends and dreams. And of the wide regions of the earth how small a part they knew. All northern peoples they called Scythians, all western Celts, without distinction. Of Africa they knew nothing but the nearest part of Ethiopia, of Asia nothing beyond the Ganges, of the vast stretches of the New World they had caught no report nor rumour. Nay, whole climates and zones, in which countless men breathe and live, were pronounced uninhabitable. The peregrinations of a Democritus, a Plato, a Pythagoras, which seemed wonderful in their eyes, were hardly more than suburban excursions. But, sons, experience is like water: the more extensive it is the freer from taint. And it is in our time, as you know, that the ocean has opened her bosom, new worlds have come to light, the limits of the old world have been thoroughly explored and studied in their distinct and special characters. If you take into consideration, then, the birth-time of your philosophy, which is, as it were, its horoscope or natal star, it is obvious the Chaldaeans could have foretold no good of it.

Now consider the men. Please acquit me of the desire to advance any far-fetched argument. I shall confine myself to what the true circumstances not only permit but demand. I find myself in fact in the fortunate position that I can speak with complete candour while preserving to them their reputation and to myself my modesty. I declare myself free of all envy and vain-glory. I contend not for the palm of wit nor lay claim to the sceptre of authority. I detract nothing from the genius of the ancients, nor from their eminence, or capacity. But I do criticise the very nature of their work, the road they took, the goal they pursued, their authority, and their findings. This is inevitable. Our belief in the riches we have inherited from them is the supreme cause of our poverty. No man can measure the extent of the injury they do to progress.

Among the ancients there are two whose findings can be drawn from their own writings – Plato and Aristotle. It would be well if this were true of some of the others. But Aristotle, like the Ottoman Turk, did not think he could reign secure till he had slain his brothers. This, though not immediately, eventually fell out as he desired. About these two, then, I must say a few words. I refrain from adding Xenophon to the list, a delightful writer and an excellent man. But those who take up philosophy, not as an anxious and laborious sphere of duty but as a sort of holiday excursion, are not for me. I restrict myself, then, to the two, Plato and Aristotle; and be it said at once that anybody who does not place them among the greatest human minds has failed in understanding or in candour. They were capacious, acute, lofty. But it remains to determine to what class of philosopher they belonged.

I recognise three classes among the philosophers of Greece. There are first the Sophists. They journeyed from one city to another, and in each place where they made a stay, they undertook, in return for a fee, to make the young men wise. Such were Gorgias, Protagoras, Hippias, whom Plato everywhere scourges and holds up to ridicule in his mocking style. For these men were not only orators and composers of speeches. They claimed to know everything. The second class, possessed of a more exalted sense of their importance, opened schools, founded or took over sects with a fixed system of beliefs, and had pupils, adherents, and successors. To this class belonged Plato, Aristotle, Zeno, Epicurus. With them we should perhaps also class Pythagoras. For he attracted pupils and founded a school of thought, though it was busy with tradition rather than disputation and nearer to a false religion than a philosophy. There was also a third class. Without noisy advertisement or professorial pomp they seriously devoted themselves to the search for truth and the study of nature. They might either (like Endymion) alone and plunged in thought philosophise for themselves, or invite a chosen few, who shared their passion, to join in the delights of their converse. They did not (like Galatea, whose delight was in the waves) expose themselves to the blustering winds of disputation. Of this sort were Empedocles, Heraclitus, Democritus, Anaxagoras, Parmenides. You will not find that these men opened schools, but they eventually reduced their speculations and discoveries to writing and so passed them on to posterity.[1]

Now, sons, you probably see what I am driving at. No matter how they reject and revile one another I regard the two first classes as closely connected in fact. I shall not shrink from telling you that I put Plato and Aristotle among the Sophists. They were Sophists of a reformed and better type, but I fail to see an essential difference. They did not journey about from place to

1. Bacon was a pioneer of research into the Presocratics, but his knowledge must not be supposed to be accurate. His disciple Vico could not distinguish Zeno the Eleatic from Zeno the Stoic, but that does not prevent his being one of the great figures in the history of thought. Bacon's ignorance of the *school* of Democritus at Abdera or that of Parmenides at Elea does not alter the validity of the distinction he seeks to draw between the professorial schools who passed on opinions to hearers from generation to generation and those whose opinions suggest an absence of 'professorial pomp' and a more serious devotion to 'the study of nature.'

place, they were free of the indignity of taking fees and from the vice of empty display. True it is, there is in them a marked solemnity and exaltation. But each headed a school, had hearers, and founded a sect. You can see for yourselves that they belong to this class.

I now turn to say something about each of these men, holding to my rule not to enter into controversy on points of doctrine but to judge by 'signs.' I begin with Aristotle, and I appeal to your memories, sons, and ask whether, in his Physics and his Metaphysics, you do not hear the voice of dialectics more often than the voice of nature. What solidity of structure can be expected from a man who constructs a world from categories? Who treats of matter and void, of rarity and density, by drawing distinctions between act and potency? Who describes the nature of the soul in terms of second intention? But these questions touch on points of doctrine, so I desist. It would be to forget myself to proceed to systematic confutation point by point, and it would be insolent to glance at the opinions of so great a man in words of mockery. But in his case the 'signs' are not good. He was of an impatient and intolerant cast of mind. He could not stay to ponder the thoughts of other men, sometimes not even his own. He was ingenious in raising objections, perpetually concerned to contradict, hostile and contemptuous of the past, and purposely obscure. Many other qualities also he had which smack of the school-master, not of the researcher into truth.

There is, of course, a reply to this. It may be said that it is easy to find fault, but, that once Aristotle's works appeared, those of many of the older thinkers were neglected and perished; that in later ages nothing better was discovered; that Aristotle was, therefore, so great a man as to dominate his predecessors and successors; and that the probability is that Philosophy reached with him its fixed and settled form. It is possible to maintain this and therefore to claim that all that now remains to be done is to preserve and polish the system of Aristotle. But for my part I regard these as the thoughts of a man either lacking in experience, or poisoned by partisanship, or just lazy. There is, as the Scripture says,[1] a kind of laziness which seems to itself to be wise and seven times weightier than reason. Without doubt, since the truth must by all means be spoken, it is precisely this laziness that inspires the greater part of this opinion. The pride innate in human nature not only finds excuses for its own vices but accords them a sort of profane reverence. To its reluctance

1. Proverbs 26, 16. Bacon seems, as usual, to quote from memory. His words are: *Est enim, ut dicit Scriptura, desidia quaedam, quae sibi prudens videtur et septemplici rationum pondere gravior.* The Vulgate runs: *Sapientior sibi piger videtur septem viris loquentibus sententias.*

to undergo the toils of research and experiment it pays the honour due to the caution which is the companion of wisdom. The nemesis is not long delayed. The indolence of individuals is mistaken for the authoritative judgment of all mankind.

There is a question we should put to ourselves. Does the fact that Aristotle drew to himself both earlier and later ages prove him truly great? Oh, great without a doubt; but no greater than the greatest of impostors. For this is the prerogative of imposture, and in especial of the Prince of imposture, the Anti-Christ. 'I am come', says the Truth Himself, 'in the name of my Father, and ye do not receive me; but, if one cometh in his own name, him ye will receive.'[1] Do ye hear, sons? Christ says that he who comes in the name of the Father, which in a true and pious, if not a literal, sense is in the name of antiquity, will not be received; but he who, levelling and destroying all that went before, usurps authority to himself and comes in his own name, him men will follow. Now if any man in philosophy ever came in his own name, Aristotle is that man. He is his own authority throughout. He so despised antiquity that he scarcely deigns to mention the name of one ancient, save to confute and revile him. Nay, he does not blush to say in round terms (which conceal a truth under their abusive form) that it is very probable that our ancestors sprang from clay or mud to judge by the foolish and earthy character of their beliefs and practices.[2]

It is not true either that the ancient philosophers, after Aristotle by the assertion of his own authority had triumphed over them, were promptly forgotten. Even in the days of the Caesars a high estimation was placed on the works of Democritus,

> whose wisdom shows
> That mighty men, destined for long to stand
> As proofs of human worth, may grace the land
> Of mutton-heads and breathe its heavy sky.[3]

It is, of course, well known that in the more civilised age of the Roman Empire many writings of the old Greeks survived intact. Though he did not lack the wish Aristotle would never have succeeded in destroying them without the aid of Attila, Genseric, and the Goths. Only then, when human

1. John 5, 43.
2. Probably a reference to *Politics* B viii, 1269a. Aristotle there says that it is probable that the earliest known men, whether earth-born or the survivors of some cataclysm, were no better than ordinary or even foolish people to day. There is nothing in the passage to justify Bacon's use of it. It is, in fact, an excellent example of Bacon's unreliability in detail.
3. Juvenal x, 48–50, on Democritus of Abdera.

learning had suffered shipwreck, did the plank of Aristotle's philosophy, being of a lighter and less solid substance, surmount the waves and, on the death of its rivals, become the accepted view.

Furthermore, the popular fancy about the worth of universal approval is unreliable and misleading. My sons, have you counted and recorded those births of time which have perished, or lain hid, or been known only in other parts of the world? Have you listed those births of time which aborted and never saw the light? Men should cease from placing on the nature of the world and the ravages of time the responsibility for their own limitations. Suppose we query the validity of men's suffrages. Suppose we deny that there is genuine agreement where men believe under compulsion and pass judgment without free consent. Men have passed from ignorance to prejudice. They have but flocked together, not agreed together. But assume that we did not entertain a universal doubt about the validity of popular judgment. Suppose our reserves touched only Aristotle himself. Would we have any reason to repent of such a healthy attitude in the midst of the mental epidemic that sweeps like the plague through mankind? Without a doubt, sons, in matters of the mind the worst of all omens is popular agreement. The situation is different in regard to religion, for there truth has come down from heaven. But in general, nothing finds favour with the many unless it strikes the imagination, like superstition, or appeals to vulgar notions, like the Sophists. So far is popular agreement of this sort from constituting a genuine and well based authority that it even raises a strong presumption to the contrary. That was well said by the Greek orator who, when met by a burst of applause, enquired: 'What have I done wrong?'[1]

But even though Aristotle were the man he is thought to be I should still warn you against receiving as oracles the thoughts and opinions of one man. What justification can there be for this self-imposed servitude? Are ye so inferior to the followers of the pagan monk, that they stopped affirming his *ipse dixit* after seven years, while you are content to repeat Aristotle's after two thousand? If zeal for antiquity had prevailed in Aristotle's day, he would never have been regarded as a great man. Are you too timid to apply to him the rule he applied to his predecessors? But, if you will be guided by me, you will deny, not only to this man but to any mortal now living or who shall live hereafter, the right to dictate your opinions. Follow men when they are right, because you have seen the light; do not follow anybody indiscriminately in everything, like blind men following a guide. You will

1. The orator was Phocion (Plutarch, *Phocion*, c. 8).

never be sorry for trusting your own strength, if you but once make trial of it. You may be inferior to Aristotle on the whole, but not in everything. Finally, and this is the head and front of the whole matter, there is at least one thing in which you are far ahead of him – in precedents, in experience, in the lessons of time. Aristotle, it is said, wrote a book in which he gathered together the laws and institutions of two hundred and fifty-five cities; yet I have no doubt that the customs and example of the single state of Rome are worth more than all of them combined, so far as military and political science are concerned. The position is the same in natural philosophy. Are you of a mind to cast aside not only your own endowments but the gifts of time? Assert yourselves before it is too late. Apply yourselves to the study of things themselves. Be not for ever the property of one man.[1]

About Plato my opinion is this. Though he avoided a political career and declined to seek public office on account of the disturbed conditions of his time, yet by natural inclination he was drawn towards political questions and devoted to them his main strength. He was not much interested in natural philosophy except in so far as it might secure his right to the noble title of philosopher and add a veneer of majesty to his ethical and political opinions. Consequently, what he wrote about nature has no foundation in fact. Rather he infected and corrupted natural studies by his theology as much as Aristotle did by his dialectic. There are excellent 'signs' in his case, if only the rest had conformed with them. He strove to win knowledge of Forms and he made use of Induction throughout, not only to establish first principles but also middle propositions. These two parts of his method, the quest for Forms and the use of Induction, are truly divine, and on their account he deserved, if he did not win, the name of divine. But he corrupted them and made them fruitless by aiming only at abstract Forms and taking the material for his Inductions only from superficial and vulgar experience. Instances of this kind, being known to everybody, are suited to discussions but not to research. Accordingly, since he did not practice serious study and observation of natural phenomena, which are the only basis of philosophy, it is no

---

1. It goes without saying that this account of Aristotle is in many particulars ill-informed. But as an effort, in the early years of the seventeenth century, to break the stranglehold of Aristotle over men's minds, with the specific end in view of making possible a fresh start in natural philosophy, it has validity. The great majority of the scientists of the age felt the need for the break. A notable exception, however, is William Harvey, whose discovery of the circulation of the blood owed much to his devotion to Aristotle, and not less to his cosmology than his biology. See Walter Pagel, *The Reaction to Aristotle in Seventeenth-Century Biological Thought* (Science, Medicine and History. Essays in Honour of Charles Singer. Vol. I, pp. 489ff.).

matter for wonder that neither his lofty genius nor his happy method accomplished much. But again I find myself slipping away from 'signs' to a consideration of his natural philosophy. A rigorous distinction, in fact, is not possible, nor, I think, has the digression displeased you.

Nay, it may perhaps be that you would like my opinion of those other philosophers known to us, not in their own writings, but through the writings of others – Pythagoras, Empedocles, Heraclitus, Anaxagoras, Democritus, Parmenides, etc. Here, my sons, I shall keep nothing back but frankly open up to you the whole of my thought. Know then that I have, with the utmost zeal and patience, sought out the slightest breath of tradition about the findings and opinions of these men. Aristotle confutes them. Plato and Cicero quote them. Plutarch devoted an essay to them. Laertius wrote their lives. The poet Lucretius sings of them. All these sources, together with various other fragments and references which can be traced, I have sought out and read, nor have I accorded them a contemptuous glance, but weighed them with patient fidelity. There can be no doubt that if their opinions, now known to us only through untrustworthy intermediaries, were extant in their own writings so that they could be drawn from the living spring, they would make an impression of much greater solidity than they now do. For the force of a theory rests on an apt harmony of mutually sustaining parts and on a rounded and complete demonstration, and is weakened when handed down piece-meal. I am convinced that, in the great variety of these opinions, there are a considerable number that have been arrived at after careful study of nature and assignment of causes. Inevitably some are better in one point, some in another. But if they be compared with Aristotle my firm conviction is that several of them penetrated more shrewdly and deeply into nature in many points than he. It was inevitable that they should do so since they were more devout devotees of experience than he. Especially is this true of Democritus, who by reason of his wide experience of the world of nature was even reputed to be a mage.

Nevertheless, if I am to hold to my resolve to deal with you candidly and without any sort of mask, I must pass over these great names with a very summary judgment. The opinions and theories of philosophers of this sort are like the plots of so many different stage-plays, contrived to present a certain degree of resemblance to reality with more or less elegance, lack of taste, or crass stupidity. And they have this further property of stage-plays that they often seem more neat, pat, and convincing than life. To be sure these earlier men were less tied to what I might call the conventions of the stage, that is to popular belief and opinion, than were Aristotle and Plato and others from the schools, and were therefore freer from ostentation and imposture, and to that extent more sane. But by and large they resembled them. All Greek philosophers, I might venture to say, were in the same boat. Their errors were various, the causes of error the same.

Nay more, I have no doubt that if power had remained in the hands of the people and of free states, the wanderings of the human mind, ever setting sail to catch the breezes of popular fancy, would never have come to a halt and confined themselves even within the limits of the mass of different speculations of which we now have knowledge. Astronomy provides an example of what I mean. Both those who accept the rotation of the earth and those who hold to the old scheme show an equal desire to 'save the appearances.' Nay, the astronomical tables suit either system. So in natural philosophy, but even more easily, can men think up theories, all differing from one another and all logically self-consistent. They all appeal to the same stock of experience, the same vulgar instances, which in the present state of philosophy exercise men's wits, but each uses them to support a different system. Even in our own age, with intellects as numbed as ours now are and in a period in which religious questions have monopolised our wits, even in our age men continue to think up new schemes of natural philosophy. Do you seek an example? Only recently Telesius of Cosenza mounted the stage and acted a new play. It had quite a plausible plot but met with little success. Gilbert of England investigated the nature of the magnet, and did so with infinite toil, and with sobriety and sound judgment in research, supporting his conclusions by a retinue, nay, by an army of experimental observations. But even he promptly showed signs of founding a new school of philosophy. His affection for Xenophanes ought to have served to caution him; some jester, you will remember, changed his name from Xenophanes (Revealer of new things) to Xenomanes (Mad about novelties). Fracastor, too, if he did not found a sect, nevertheless exercised his right to a theory of his own. So did Cardan, a thinker of less weight.

Now I imagine, sons, that you are bewildered at hearing from me this sweeping rejection of opinions and authorities. You have, perhaps, a good opinion of me but yet doubt your ability to sustain along with me the invidiousness of such a stand. Very probably you are wondering and weighing up in your own minds what my ultimate intention is, and what kind of proposition I am about to put before you. I shall keep you no longer in suspense. I hope, unless indeed my proposal is felt to be quite unfair, that it will free you from wonder and me from reproach. You will not have forgotten the suggestion I made at the outset, that the ancients should retain undiminished and unimpaired, not their authority and credit (for that is ruinous), but the honour and reverence in which they are held. For while we might exercise the right, common to all men, to criticise and reject, according to the best of our judgment, any discovery or theory of theirs we find to be wrong, mercifully that is not necessary. By a lucky dispensation we can avoid contradicting them and thus escape the ill-feeling it provokes.

Listen then, sons, while I explain this point. I profess to have something better to offer you than the ancients. If I did this while pursuing the same path as they, then by no verbal ingenuity could I avoid challenging them in intellect, excellence, or capacity. Not that that would be improper or unprecedented. It would merely expose me to an unequal contest, for I have no illusion about my inferiority both to the men of old and the men of the present day. But, to put the matter simply before you, in as much as a lame man on the road will outstrip an athlete who is off it, the case is altered. Frankly, then, without artifice or pretence, I state my case, and this is it: If all the wits of all the ages were combined, then, if they continued to pursue their present path, that is to say, the method of mental cogitation and argument, they could make no great advances in the sciences. Nor is this all. I add further that the more intelligent a man is, if he too soon deserts the light of nature, that is to say, the enquiry into particulars and the evidence drawn therefrom, the more steeply does he plunge into the obscure and tortuous recesses and caverns of the imagination and the more difficult does he make it to get out.

You cannot have failed, sons, to read the lesson of the scholastic philosophers. What acuteness, what strength of intellect, these men had! Yet what spiders' webs they wove for us, wonderful for their texture and the fineness of their thread, but useless for any practical purpose! They had too much leisure for meditation and ran to seed, and, like animals kept in seclusion in the dark, they became quarrelsome.

Then consider this further advantage of my way. My system and method of research is of such a nature that it tends to equalise men's wits and capacities, like the holdings of the Spartans. If a man, relying only on the steadiness of his hand or the keenness of his eye, tries to draw a straight line or describe a perfect circle, then everything depends on hand or eye. But, give him a straight-edge or a compass, and it is no longer so. Similarly, in that kind of natural philosophy which rests solely on intellectual strength, one man may far outdistance another. In the kind I recommend intellectual differences between men count for little more than such differences as commonly exist in their senses. For my part I am emphatically of the opinion that men's wits require not the addition of feathers and wings, but of leaden weights. Men are very far from realising how strict and disciplined a thing is research into truth and nature, and how little it leaves to the judgment of men.[1]

But it must not be thought either that I am introducing to you something far-fetched or mysterious, some god-from-the-machine. Our way might properly be described as *literate experience*, the art or plan for an honest interpretation of nature, a true path from sense to intellect.[2]

Do you not now, sons, perceive what is accomplished by my proposals? In the first place the ancients retain their due honour. In what depends upon intellect and meditation they showed themselves wonderfully proficient. I do not think that we, by following their path, could do nearly so well. Secondly, you will not miss my point, that this wholesale rejection of authorities is much less invidious than to reject some and approve others. That would have been to execute judgment upon them; but actually all I am doing is, as I have said, to point out a new way. Finally, you see plainly

1. These opinions, expressed also elsewhere by Bacon, have caused much misunderstanding. He did not think every Tom, Dick, or Harry could be a scientist. The constitution of Solomon's House in his *New Atlantis*, and passage after passage in his other writings, make clear how rare a thing in his opinion a great scientist was. Humble as he was about his own capacities, at the end of his life, when he was trying single-handed, in his *Sylva Silvarum*, to make an encyclopaedia of factual knowledge to serve as a basis for a genuine natural philosophy, he lamented that he, who might have aspired to the role of an architect, was compelled to fill that of a hod-man. The aim of his remarks was very different. He is trying to clip the wings of speculation which is not weighted by attention to observed particulars, and to insist that masses of detailed observation, such as are within the capacity of very many people, are the necessary basis of progress.

2. Literate experience or learned experience (*literata experientia*) is one of the most fundamental and fruitful of Bacon's conceptions. It is a definite stage in advance beyond the experience implicitly embodied in techniques but unrecorded and therefore not available for independent theoretical development. It might be described as the intellectualising of the industrial process, the emergence of science proper out of a merely economic activity, as a stage in history and a stage in thought. It includes (i) the recording of experience and, arising out of that, (ii) the employment of a certain direction and order in experiment. It does not include Bacon's next step, (iii) the ascent to Axioms or First Principles. Cf. Anderson, *Op cit.*, pp. 284–8; and for other occurrences of the phrase in Bacon see *N.O.* 1, 101, where it is used in the first sense; *De Aug.* v, 2, where it is used in the second sense; and *C. et V.*, 18. Spedding also has an excellent note, 1, 623.

what is reserved for myself, whether by my own claim or by the allowance of others. It is not any great glory of intellect, excellence, or capacity, but just good fortune – and that too rather yours than mine, since my plan is rather fruitful in use than remarkable as a discovery. Perhaps you wonder how I came to think of it. For my part, I am astonished that nobody thought of it long ago. How could it happen that no mortal man devoted head and heart to providing helps and support for the human mind in studying nature and sifting the experience thus acquired? To think of the whole process of discovery and invention being left to the obscurity of tradition, the giddy whirl of argument, the billows of chance, and the devious course of mere experience! To think that nobody succeeded in opening up a middle way between practical experience and unsupported theorising!

But there is really no cause for wonder. There is no lack of evidence of a certain ill-conditioned awkwardness of the human mind which makes it begin by distrusting and go on to despise itself. At first it seems impossible that such and such a thing should ever be discovered; once it has been discovered, the wonder is that it remained undiscovered so long. The real truth is that the obstacle to the course I propose lies not in its obscurity or its difficulty, but in human pride. Nature herself in great part, nay, in her best part, is despised by man. It is this pride that has brought men to such a pitch of madness that they prefer to commune with their own spirits rather than with the spirit of nature. They imagine that arts are *made* by them, not *discovered*.

Your education, my sons, might be compared to a conducted tour through a portrait-gallery of the ancients. Very probably you have not failed to observe that a certain portion of the gallery was cut off by a curtain. Behind that curtain lie the secrets of .that antiquity which preceded the learning of the Greeks. But why should you wish to direct my attention to those remote ages, of which the true history and even the traces of that history have vanished? Is not that remote antiquity like the poet's description of Fame, hiding her head in the clouds and relating wonders, singing in the same breath of what was done and never done.[1] Well I know, if I wished to be insincere, that it would not be difficult to make men believe that among the sages of old, long before Greek times, philosophy and the sciences flourished with greater value and less noise. If I did this I could, by referring my present proposals to those ancient times, invest them with a certain solemnity, as self-made men do, who attach to themselves the nobility of

1. Vergil, *Aeneid* IV, 173–90.

some ancient stock by means of genealogical hints and conjectures.[1] But my resolution is fixed, to rely on the evidence of facts and avoid any sort of imposture, however convenient or attractive. Accordingly I shall not interject into the present discussion my judgment on those centuries. I shall just remark in passing that, though the fables of the poets are of a nature to lend themselves to many interpretations, I should be loth to draw recondite meanings out of them, if they were invented by those who have handed them on to us. But this, I think, is not so. They are not offered to us as new inventions now for the first time brought forward, but as things formerly believed and known. This circumstance increases their value in my eyes, since it suggests that they are the sacred survivals of better times. But, however that may be, it has no vital bearing on the matter in hand. It may well be that my project, and much greater projects than mine, were really known to remote antiquity. But this is of no importance for the business in hand. Similarly no practical importance attaches to the debate whether the New World is the old Atlantis and was known to the ancients or whether it has now been discovered for the first time. Truth must be discovered by the light of nature, not recovered from the darkness of the past.

Now, sons, even if it be something more than you have bargained for, I must take leave to offer you my views on the philosophy of the alchemists. The fact is that your philosophy, by being strong in arguments and weak in

1. This passage, including what follows, is essential for the understanding of *De Sapientia Veterum*; written and published in the very next year, it seems to do precisely what he here says he will not do. A careful weighing of all Bacon says will acquit him of any disingenuity. He had two ends in view – one, to found the philosophy of works, the other, to overcome the resistance to it in the public mind. A discussion of the old fables, useless for the first purpose, could be made to serve the second. The circumstances of the age, which was intensely interested in the genuine problem of the meaning of the fabulous and legendary past, combined with Bacon's own conviction that there was more in the problem than meets the eye, opened up the possibility of a work which would be fashionable, which would not be unworthy of his consideration, and which would give him the chance to produce another 'mixture of old and new' to prepare the way for 'the new unmixed.' So came to birth *The Wisdom of the Ancients*, a composition of great wit, charm, and feeling, in which the ancient fables are made to disclose the thoughts nearest to his heart: the need for a cessation of religious wars and religious disputes; the real possibility of a revolution in the conditions of human life by the creation of a natural philosophy productive of works; the superiority of the atomism of Democritus to any other view of nature as a general base for science; the inevitable destructiveness of material progress unless governed by charity. The work was much praised and widely read. There is, in short, every reason to believe that it did effectively what Bacon intended it to do, namely prepare the way for acceptance of his full philosophy. During the seventeenth century there were nine editions of the Latin original, five editions in English, two in French, and one in German.

works, has produced in some quarters a high regard for alchemy. And, when we consider the practice of the alchemists, we may agree that its merits are well hit off in the familiar story of the old man and his sons. He bequeathed to them, you remember, a treasure of gold buried in his vineyard in some spot unknown. They put their backs into the work, dug up the vineyard and, though they found no gold, made it productive. It is the same with the sons of chemistry. There may or may not be gold buried in nature's field, but at least, by their laborious digging, by their activity and persistence, they have done much to further and assist mankind. They have endowed human life and fortunes with many discoveries not to be despised.

Nevertheless the worth of their speculative philosophy is slight and deceptive. You have heard of the spoiled boy who found a plank on the strand and dreamed of building himself a ship. Such are the alchemists. They are in love with their art, possessed with the ambition to base a whole philosophy on a few experiments made in their furnaces. This kind of theorising is more easily and openly convicted of vanity than that already discussed, which has the advantage of greater sobriety and discretion. For the commonly held philosophy traverses the whole field of nature and samples a little of almost everything, and is therefore better able to defend itself in the eyes of most men. But a man who fabricates a complete system out of a limited range of experiments to which he has become accustomed, is both in fact more mistaken and in appearance more trivial. This, in my view, is the truth about alchemy.

The basis of their philosophy on which its theoretical structure is raised is this. There are four matrices or elements in nature in which the various seeds or species of things mature their offspring. These, when they come to birth, are quadriform to match each of the elements. Consequently in sky, air, water, earth, nothing exists without some conjugate or parallel in the other three. Even man himself they have turned into a pantomime or universal mimic, a combination of all elements, by a misapplication of the choice term *microcosm*. This fanciful construction secures the allegiance of no competent judge. I do not think any genuine natural philosopher would admit even into his dreams such an arbitrary ordering of nature.[1] But, to conclude what I began to say, alchemy is involved in an error which is the reverse of the current philosophy. The current philosophy, out of its vast

---

1. Bacon has not managed to be as clear as might be wished. The four elements are fire, air, water and earth; the four matrices mercury, sulphur, arsenic and salt. Four fundamental processes, combustion, evaporation, solution, condensation match the four elements.

stock, takes but little to serve as material for invention, alchemy from its tiny stock takes much. For my part I am here content to let Paracelsus speak for me (it may be conjectured that he has a loud voice) and celebrate and proclaim that Light of Nature on which he loves to insist.[1]

Mention of alchemy draws me on to add a word about natural magic, an art which now dishonours its solemn and all but holy name. This art is usually held in honour by alchemists; but it is beneath condemnation on an occasion like the present. Its worthlessness protects it. What can that art have to do with us whose dogmas are but shameless fancy and superstition, whose works but conjuring and imposture? If in the midst of its endless deceits it does produce some genuine effect, it is only such as to excite wonder at its novelty not anything either intended or fitted to serve any useful purpose. Investigate a piece of magic and you are more than likely to find, as the naughty poet sings, that 'the least part of the girl is herself.'[2] The mark of genuine science is that its explanations take the mystery out of things. Imposture dresses things up to seem more wonderful than they would be without the dress. Yet this vain philosophy is both despised and received, though it is the sort of apothecary's shop which prescribes ragwort as a remedy for lust and fox-lungs for phthisis![3]

But enough about the claims of magic. They would not be worth attention even if they were as innocent as they are absurd. Let us resume the main thread of our discourse and proceed to test the received philosophy in the light of our 'signs'. The digression was justified as an attempt to prepare your minds, which is the business now in hand. For it is a fact than when, by good fortune, anything new is brought forward, the mind rejects it by reason of a twofold prejudice. On the one hand there is the inveterate belief in established views. On the other hand is an erroneous anticipation or prefiguration of the new proposal. It is assumed to rest on something long since condemned and rejected, or, at the best, to tend towards something justly scorned for its triviality or absurdity. Let us then retrace our steps and examine the 'signs'. There is no 'sign' more certain and more noble than that from fruits. In religion we are warned that faith be shown by works. It is

1. The remark about Paracelsus having a loud voice seems no more than a poor and tasteless play on his name, which suggests *paraclete*, i.e. advocate, comforter.

2. Ovid, *Remedia Amoris*, 333-4, of the girl who is all make-up.

3. Pliny in his *Natural History* says (XXVI, 63) that ragwort (*satyrion*) was an aphrodisiac and (XXVIII, 57) that the lungs of the fox, dried over a slow fire and taken with water, cured the spleen. The point of Bacon's remark is that both of these magical remedies are misapplied.

altogether right to apply the same test to philosophy. If it be barren let it
be set at naught. All the more should this be so if, instead of the fruits of
grape or olive, it bear the thistles and thorns of disputes and contentions.
Only too aptly do the words of the poet apply to your philosophy. I think
first of the words:

> The cursed darnel and barren oat prevail[1]

and again of this:

> And girt were her white loins with yelping dogs.[2]

Yea, from afar your philosophy seems a comely maid; but it is only in the
upper half. At a cursory glance, she is not without charm or allure. But
come to a more nice survey. Consider the belly and the womb and the hope
of fruit thereof. Then, in place of those works and that power of action
which are the worthy and legitimate fruit of mental endeavour, what find
you but those howling, barking mouths, made notorious by the shipwreck
of so many intellects?

Now the begetter of this evil is Aristotle, but your philosophy is its nurse.
He entertained himself and sought renown by bringing up questions of
little practical importance and then disposing of them. Very well; the
reputation he deserves is that of a contriver of contradictions, not of a cham-
pion of truth. But his wretched example was copied and a scientific education now consists of posing problems and supplying answers. It is different
if a man establishes some point, proves it, gives it shape and reveals its
bearings. Such a man keeps misunderstandings and objections at a distance.
In a sense he prevents their arising or drives them away before they can
approach. But to quarrel over every detail is to conclude nothing but sow
for ever the seeds of fresh dispute. Let a man set up in the midst some one
clear source of light and truth, he will not then need to carry his pale candles
of confutation into every nook and corner of error, resolving a few puzzles,
but bringing to light, and, I might say, creating as many more by his very
method of dealing with error. But this is just what Aristotle aimed at. He
wanted to provide men with some ready-made solution for every problem,
some answer to give, some way out of every difficulty, not some deep conviction, some crystal clear thought, some true knowledge. And your philosophy is so true to its author that it fixes and eternises the questions he first

1. Vergil, *Georgics* I, 154.   2. Vergil, *Aeneid* VI, 75, of Scylla.

raised. The judgment of Nasica prevails over that of Cato.[1] The aim of your philosophy is not in the course of time to kill those doubts, which are the enemy, and to press on into new spheres of knowledge, but to suffer those everlasting 'problems', which are our Carthage, to keep us always in trim for a fresh debate.

As the next 'sign' take the question of an abundant harvest of works. I say that your philosophy – and it is a field which has been tilled and cultivated for ages – has not yielded one achievement tending to enrich and relieve man's estate, which can truthfully be set down to the credit of its speculations. So true is this that it might be claimed that the instinct of dumb beasts has produced more results than the discourses of learned men.[2] Celsus, like a wise and candid man, admits that the practice of medicine came first and that it was only later that men began to philosophise about it and seek out and assign causes. The reverse was not the case. Experience was not derived from philosophy and the study of causes. Nor is this all. Your philosophy would have deserved well of practice, even though it could add nothing to experimental knowledge, if it had made practice more strict and prudent (which is perhaps its function) and had not rather blocked its growth and progress. The truly damaging and disastrous fact is, not that it does not produce discoveries, but that it crushes and extinguishes them.

Aristotle's doctrine of the four elements is a case in point. It is, to be sure, but a gross and obvious thing, for bodies of this sort are seen in vast number and bulk. Moreover he did not originate it, but merely lent it his authority. The originator was Empedocles, by whom it was better put. But it was later snapped up by the doctors and served as a pattern for further groups of four – four temperaments, four humours, four primary qualities. Thereafter it may truly be said that like some baleful inauspicious star it brought immeasurable sterility on medicine and many mechanical arts. Men satisfied themselves with such neat compendious trifles, substituted them for fresh and fruitful observations of facts, and gave themselves no further trouble. If, then, the saying be true, *By their fruits ye shall know them*, what more remains to be said?[3]

1. The reference here is to Plutarch's *Cato*, xxvii. There we read: 'On whatever topic he spoke Cato ended with the words *Carthage must be destroyed*. Nasica ended all his speeches with the counter-plea *Carthage must be spared*.'
2. This is not so extravagant as it may seem. Tradition reports many medical discoveries drawn from observation of animal behaviour. In Bacon's own day Dr Jacquinto, the Queen's physician, went down to Essex, to learn from the sheep – with splendid results (Aubrey's *Lives*, ed. by Dick, p. xxiii).   3. Luke 6, 44.

Come now, sons, and examine the 'signs' drawn from progress. That philosophy of yours is like a plant torn up by the roots. Had it remained firm-rooted in the lap and womb of nature and been nourished therefrom, that could never have come about which for the space of two thousand years has been observed, namely that the abstract sciences should have remained at the same level of development and gained no notable increase. Polished they may have been by an individual here and there, furbished up and put in better trim (such improvements may be set against the rending, distortion, and smirching they have suffered from countless hands); but in no way has their scope been widened nor their content increased. In the mechanical arts, however, a different spectacle meets the eye. As if animated by some spirit they grow and flourish. At first rude, next serviceable, then choice, they are always on the move. But philosophy and the theoretical sciences, like statues of the gods, are thronged with worshippers, but never move. Nay, often they attain their full bloom with their first author and then begin to wither and droop.

Nor is it a matter for surprise that mechanical arts and philosophy should differ in this way. In the former the wits of individuals mingle, in the latter they corrupt and destroy one another. The mistake is to suppose that in the sciences there is a fixed upper-limit of attainment, and that this, as a rule, is reached within the life-span of a single individual, who, profiting by the circumstances of the time, becomes the leader of his age, examines and appraises all other writers, and thus brings the sciences to a definitive and absolute perfection. After him later writers can aspire only to the second rank of expositors and rearrangers of the works of the master, adapting them to the requirements of their time. If anybody imagines this to be the case, let him realise that he assigns to human affairs a greater degree of foresight, order, and good luck than the facts admit. Human affairs do, indeed, admit of luck, but human vanity turns even windfalls to no good. But this, in truth, is how the matter stands. Every science grows by the patient observation of many men, one grasping one truth one another, as different aspects of the subject are seriously handled and essayed. But sooner or later up starts some self-confident fellow, eloquent of speech, popular in method, who gathers all the individual contributions into one body according to his private fancy and hands it on to posterity. In the process much is corrupted and deformed. It can be taken for granted that all the more arduous and noble speculations will be omitted as immoderate and far-fetched. Then posterity in its turn, rejoiced to find the subject so simple and compact, falls to congratulating itself on its good fortune, assumes those servile roles to which I have referred, and abandons research. Yet it is an unchallengeable truth, my sons, that knowledge which is founded in nature has, like living waters, perpetual uprushings and outflowings, while knowledge based on opinion can, of course, vary but never increase.

We have also another 'sign', although I am not sure if 'sign' is here the right word. Rather we have to do with a testimony, and that the most valid of all testimonies, to wit, the confession and verdict of the authors on whom you rely. These very men, who have seized the dictatorship in the sciences and make such bold pronouncements, yet, every now and then, when they come to themselves, turn to lamenting the subtlety of nature, the obscurity of things, the feebleness of the human understanding, and so forth. But you must not make the mistake, sons, of ascribing these complaints to modesty or humility, which are the most blessed of all virtues in matters intellectual. The contrary is true. This profession, or proclamation, for I cannot call it a confession, most assuredly takes its rise in pride, in envy, and in other motives of this sort. What they intend is simply this, that whatever in the sciences is unknown by them or untouched by their masters, should be firmly declared to be beyond the limits of the possible. Such is their modesty, such is their humility. And the sorry state of science is the result. In the pinched and narrow state of human fortunes nothing is for the present more to be deplored or of more evil omen for the future than this practice I am describing. To rescue their ignorance from ignominy they transform the feebleness of their art into a calumny on nature. Whatever their art cannot attain they are artful enough to dub impossible. And to be sure their art is safe from condemnation so long as it judges its own case.

From this source spring various opinions and pronouncements of the philosophers. These pronouncements have no other sense or purpose than to promote a deliberate and artificial despair both as regards the acquisition of knowledge and the possibility of action. They are a shameful device for safeguarding the honour and glory of their art. To this end the Academics made a cult of the incomprehensibility of nature and condemned mankind to eternal darkness.[1] The same end was served by the doctrine that Forms (that is, the true differences of things) are indiscoverable. The intention was to keep men walking up and down for ever in nature's forecourt without ever paving a way into her palace. To the same purpose were those ill-

1. Cf. *N.O.* I, 126. The New or Second Academy under Arcesilaus (315–241 B.C.) and Carneades (214–129 B.C.) was noted for its scepticism.

founded views on the absolute distinction between the heat of the sun and the heat of fire, and on the limitation of men's power to the mere juxtaposition of things and the reservation to nature alone of the power to make a true combination. Like Vulcan with Minerva, art was never to aspire to woo Nature and win her over. I could find many more examples of the eagerness of these authorities to proclaim their own weakness and their will to repress the enterprise of others. How can I advise you, then, my sons, however well-disposed and obliging you may feel towards me, to entangle your fortunes in enterprises not only now despaired of but condemned in advance never to succeed? But my time is running out, sons, and I am tempted by my love of you and of the business in hand, to take up one topic after another. I yearn for some secret of initiation which, like the coming of April or of Spring, might avail to thaw and loosen your fixed and frozen minds.

It remains to treat of the most certain of all 'signs'. Methods of procedure are potentially things themselves. I mean that the value of any thing or effect will be determined by the value of the method of production. Now if the methods followed in the constitution of your philosophy are not the right ones, if they cannot pass the test, obviously the hopes you cherish of a good result will be proved vain. Let us imagine, sons, that some enormous obelisk was to be moved to grace a triumph or for some other occasion of splendour, and suppose the attempt was made with the naked hands, would you not think this mad?[1] Suppose now the contractors increased the number of workers and hoped to succeed in this way, would you not think them madder still? Suppose next they held a review and cast out the weaker labourers and relied only on the strong and vigorous as the best means of attaining their end. Disappointed in this, suppose they took counsel of the art of athletics and refused to let any of the workers turn up before their hands, arms, and sinews had been well oiled and otherwise treated by their trainers, would you not protest that they were resolved on continuing to be mad on a planned and rational basis? A similar demented zeal inspires our intellectual efforts. Men apply their naked, or unaided, intellect to the task. From the mere number or quality of the minds engaged they hope great things. By dialectics, the athletic art of the mind, they strengthen their mental sinews. But they do not bring in machines to multiply and combine their individual efforts. And, as due aids are not supplied to the mind, so

1. Probably a topical reference. Domenico Fontana (1543–1607) erected four obelisks in Rome between 1586 and 1589. The scene was represented in fresco in the Vatican Library and described by himself in a treatise of date 1589.

nature is studied without due attention. How can we deny it? Does founding a philosophy involve nothing more than passing judgment on nature in the light of a few superficial and commonplace experiments and then spending whole ages meditating on the results? I had not supposed, sons, that we were on such familiar terms with nature that, in response to a casual and perfunctory salutation, she would condescend to unveil for us her mysteries and bestow on us her blessings.

Or let me change the image. It seems to me that men look down and study nature as from some remote and lofty tower. Nature presents to their gaze a certain picture of herself, or a cloudy semblance of a picture, in which all the minute differences of things, on which the practice and prosperity of men rest, are blurred by distance. So men toil and strive, straining the eyes of the mind, fixing their gaze in prolonged meditation, or shifting it about to get things into better focus. Finally they construct the arts of disputation, like ingenious perspective glasses, in order to seize and master the subtle differences of nature. A ridiculous kind of ingenuity, is it not, and misdirected energy for a man to climb his tower, arrange his lenses, and screw up his eyes to get a closer view, when he might avoid all that laborious contrivance and tedious industry and achieve his end by a way, not only easy, but far superior in its benefits and utility, namely by getting down from his tower and coming close to things?[1] Ridiculous I have called it, but all the same it is the way we use our minds. We have no right, sons, to expect nature to come to us. Enough if, on our approaching her with due respect, she condescends to show herself.

Now it may occur to some of you that the ancients also, Aristotle included, must have had a similar programme. You will say they must have begun their meditations by preparing a vast collection of examples and particular facts, and that therefore they entered upon and carried through the project I am proposing to you as a novelty. If we attempt it, we shall be doing it over again. My sons, this is certainly not a sound view. They themselves put forward their own plan and method of enquiry. Their writings remain to give us an accurate picture of it. What they did was this. They started from worthless inductions and jumped at once to conclusions of the highest

1. It is too early for Bacon to have the telescope in mind. What he is thinking of is an arrangement of lenses and mirrors of the kind Thomas Digges (*Stratioticos*, 1579, pp. 189–90) says his father Leonard devised: '. . . He was able by perspective glasses duly situated upon convenient angles to discover every particularity in the country round about, wheresoever the sun-beams might pierce.' Quoted from Crombie, *Grosseteste and Experimental Science*, p. 279. Spelling modernised.

generality. These they took as the poles on which their world of discourse revolved; everything else they adapted to conform with these fixed and changeless truths. Their science having been established in this fashion, when a controversy arose over any example or instance, as being in contradiction to their views, they did not take steps to revise their theories. No; they retained the theory and brought the unruly facts into order. This they did either by some subtle dialectical distinction or (since they were not such bad fellows after all) they let it stand as an exception. At other times it was not the resolving of a contradiction but the explanation of some obscure fact that was required. This they managed either by ingeniously finding a place for it in their speculative scheme or by torturing it out of its true form. The whole of this enterprise and effort I regard as baseless.

Do not, then, be deceived, if you find quite frequently in some of Aristotle's writings mention of observations and particulars. You are to understand that it comes too late, after his mind was made up. His practice was not to seek information from unfettered experiment but to exhibit experience captive and bound. He did not introduce a wide impartial survey of experience to assist his investigation of truth; he brought in a carefully schooled and selected experience to justify his pronouncements.

I must warn you against another misunderstanding. Do not imagine that the fine differences of things which I so much desire to discover are identical with the distinctions of the scholastics and are brilliantly exemplified in them. Do not imagine that this belated subtlety can remedy the initial negligence, haste, and rash judging. Rather believe that what is said of Time is true of nature. Nature must be taken by the forelock, being bald behind. All this tardy subtlety and meticulous care after the time for observation is gone permits one only to clutch at Nature, never to lay hold of her and capture her. Of one thing I am confident, and you will soon find it out for yourselves as you gradually become accustomed to the genuine native subtlety of things. When you actually experience by observation the minute differences of things, when they are either laid bare to sense or forced into the light by evidence which can be submitted to sense, I am confident you will then regard that other subtlety of disputations and of words, which has now captivated your imagination and taken possession of your minds, as a thing absurd, a kind of evil spirit or magic charm.

Let us, then, bid goodbye to these abstract philosophies, and let us, you and I, my sons, take our stand by reality. Let us not set our minds on the idle glory of founding a sect but in a spirit of responsibility concern ourselves with the task of promoting utility and greatness. Let us establish a chaste and lawful marriage between Mind and Nature, with the divine mercy as bride-woman. And let us pray God, the Father of men and nature as well as of lights and consolations, by Whose power and will these things are done, that from that marriage may issue, not monsters of the imagination, but a race of heroes to subdue and extinguish such monsters, that is to say, whole-some and useful inventions to war against our human necessities and, so far as may be, to bring relief therefrom. Let this be our prayer at the consumma-tion of this rite.

Now, sons, all are agreed that the arts and sciences fall under one of two categories, the empirical and the rational. What we have not been allowed to see till now is the proper mingling of the two. The Empirics, like ants, gather and consume. The Rationalists, like spiders, spin webs out of them-selves. The Bee adopts the middle course, drawing her material from the flowers of the garden or the field, but transforming it by a faculty peculiar to herself. Such should be the activity of a genuine philosophy. It should draw its material from natural history and mechanical experience, but not take it unaltered into the memory, but digest and assimilate it for storing in the understanding. Look then for this gift of celestial honey, and say not, with the sluggard, *There is a lion in the path*.[1] Shake off the chains which oppress you and be masters of yourselves. Second only to your own merit, surely nothing can give you greater courage than reflection on the enterprise, good fortune, and great exploits of our own age. Not for nothing have we opposed our modern 'There is more beyond' to the 'Thus far and no further' of antiquity. The thunderbolt is inimitable, said the ancients. In defiance of them we have proclaimed it imitable, and that not wildly but like sober men, on the evidence of our new engines. Nay, we have succeeded in imitating the heaven, whose property it is to encircle the earth; for this we have done by our voyages. It would disgrace us, now that the wide spaces of the material globe, the lands and seas, have been broached and explored, if the limits of the intellectual globe should be set by the narrow discoveries of the ancients. Nor are those two enterprises, the opening up of the earth and the opening up of the sciences, linked and yoked together in any trivial way. Distant voyages and travels have brought to light many things in nature, which may throw fresh light on human philosophy and science and correct by experience the opinions and conjectures of the ancients. Not only reason but prophecy connects the two. What else can the prophet mean who, in speaking about

1. Proverbs 26, 13.

the last times, says: Many will pass through and knowledge will be multiplied?[1] Does he not imply that the passing through or perambulation of the round earth and the increase or multiplication of science were destined to the same age and century?

Witness also the art of printing, unknown to the ancients. By it the discoveries of one man can pass like a flash of lightning and be promptly shared, thus stimulating zeal and effecting an interchange of ideas. We should avail ourselves of the advantages of our times and see to it that in the midst of so many favourable circumstances we ourselves do not fail. As for me, sons, having taken the first step by way of preparation of your minds, I shall not fail·you in what must follow. Well I know that the tablets of the mind are not like ordinary writing-tablets. On them you can write nothing till you have expunged the old; in the mind you cannot expunge the old except by writing in the new. Accordingly I shall make no long delay. I only give you this advice, that you do not promise yourself such great things from my discoveries as not to expect better from your own. I foresee for myself a destiny like that of Alexander, ... now pray, do not accuse me of vanity till you have heard me out. While his memory was fresh his exploits were regarded as portents. Of the orators who vied with one another to praise him one said: 'We no longer live like mortal men, but have been born to this destiny that men should speak portents of us.' But when admiration had cooled and men looked more closely into the matter, note the sober judgment passed upon him by the Roman historian: 'All Alexander did was dare to despise shams.'[2] Something like this later generations will say of me. Emancipated, masters of themselves, having learned by experience their own powers, they will forge far ahead of my first steps. In the verdict they pass on me they will be right to deny that anything I have done is great. But they will be wrong if they ascribe to daring what is due to humility, to humility, I say,

---

1. Daniel 12, 4. An excellent example of Bacon's practice of quoting from memory. The Vulgate says *Plurimi pertransibunt et multiplex erit scientia.* Here he writes *Multi,* etc., changing only one word. But in the frontispiece to the *Instauratio Magna,* where one might expect special care, he rewrites *Multi pertransibunt et augebitur scientia.* The quotation also reveals his attitude to biblical prophecy, which is the same as Newton's but more sober and discreet. In *Valerius Terminus* (Sp. III, 221) Bacon had called this 'a special prophecy appointed to this autumn of the world.' Later the notion of the autumn of the world fades out. In *Instauratio Magna* Bacon gives to this oracle a more precise application. The passing through is made to refer to the Pillars of Hercules and foretells the escape from the Mediterranean Sea (and ancient civilisation) to the oceans of the world and a new epoch of human history. This later interpretation is here beginning to emerge.

2. Livy IX, 17.

and to the absence of that human pride which has ruined all by conferring the title sacred upon certain fleeting meditations instead of reserving it for the divine signature on things. Here only do I felicitate myself, only on this account do I hold myself happy and well-deserving of the human race, that I have shown the power inherent in a true and proper humbling of the human spirit. But it is for others to decide what they owe to me. I owe myself and all I have to you.

*   *   *

All those present pronounced the address worthy of the greatness of the human race and name, and deserving to be called candid rather than arrogant. They talked to one another saying that they were like men who had come suddenly out of thick shade into the open light and were for the moment dazzled, but carried with them a sure and happy augury of better sight to come.

Then the narrator asked me what I had to say to it. 'I am happy', I said, 'at what you had to tell.' 'Then', said he, 'if, as you say, you like it, will you, when you write on these matters, find room to include my report and not suffer the fruit of my travels to perish.' 'A fair request', said I, 'and I shall not forget.'

BIBLIOGRAPHY

Agricola, Georgius, *De Re Metallica*, Libri XII. Basileae, MDLVI.

Agrippa, Cornelius, *Three Books of Occult Philosophy*. Translated by J. F., London, 1651.

Anderson, Fulton H., *The Philosophy of Francis Bacon*. Univ. of Chicago Press, 1948.

Andrewes, Lancelot, *Sermons*. Oxford, 1841.

Blackbourne, John, F. *Baconi Opera Omnia*. IV vols, London, MDCCXXX.

Bodin, Jean, *Methodus ad facilem Historiarum Cognitionem*. Amsterdam, 1650.

Bodley, Sir Thomas, *Letter to Francis Bacon on Cogitata et Visa* (Trecentale Bodleianum. Clarendon Press, 1913).

Brewer, J. S., *Roger Bacon's Opus Tertium*. London, 1859.

Campbell, W. E., *Erasmus, Tyndale and More*. London, 1949.

Caspari, F., *Humanism and the Social Order in Tudor England*. Univ. of Chicago Press, 1954.

Cave, William, *Scriptorum Ecclesiasticorum Historia Literaria*. Geneva, 1705.

Conti, Natale, *Mythologia*. Venice, 1551.

Crombie, A. C., *Augustine to Galileo: The History of Science A.D. 400–165*. London, 1952.

Grosseteste and the Origins of Experimental Science, 1100–1750. Oxford, 1953.

Curtis, Mark H., *Oxford and Cambridge in Transition, 1558–1642*. Clarendon Press. 1959.

Dick, O. L., *Aubrey's Brief Lives*. London, 1958.

Farrington, B., *Francis Bacon: Philosopher of Industrial Science*. Abelard-Schuman, New York, 1947.

On Misunderstanding the Philosophy of Francis Bacon (Science, Medicine and History. Essays in Honour of Charles Singer. Vol. I, pp. 439–450). Oxford, 1953.

Gardiner, S., article on Francis Bacon (*Dictionary of National Biography*).

Gilbert, Sir Humphrey, *Queen Elizabeth's Academy* (Early English Text Society, 1869).

Gruter, Isaac, F. *Baconi Scripta in . . . Philosophia*. Amsterdam, 1653. (First publication of text of *Temporis Partus Masculus* and *Cogitata et Visa*.)

Hatch, Edwin, *The Influence of Greek Ideas on Christianity*. Hibbert Lecture, 1888.

Lagarde, A. (pseudonym of Turmel, J.), *The Latin Church in the Middle Ages*. Edinburgh, 1915.

Lipschutz, A. *Tres Medicos Contemporaneos*. Buenos Aires, 1958.

BIBLIOGRAPHY

Maritain, J., *An Introduction to Philosophy*. London, 1932.

Mondolfo, R., *En los Origines de la Filosofia de la Cultura*. Buenos Aires, 1960.

Montagu, Basil, *The Works of Francis Bacon*. 16 vols, London, 1825–36.

Nef, John U., *Industry and Government in France and England 1540–1640*. (Mem. of the Amer. Phil. Soc., 1940, xv).

Pagel, W., *Paracelsus*. Basle and New York, 1958.

The Reaction to Aristotle in Seventeenth-Century Biological Thought (Science, Medicine and History. Essays in honour of Charles Singer. Vol. i, p. 489ff.). Oxford, 1953.

Palissy, B., *Discours Admirables*. Paris, 1580.

Parry, R. St John, *Henry Jackson, a Memoir*. Cambridge, 1926.

Read, Conyers, *Lord Burghley and Queen Elizabeth*. London, 1960.

Rossi, Manlio, *Per il progresso della scienza*. Milan, 1934.

Rossi, Paolo, *La Nuova Atlantide e Altri Scritti di F. Bacone*. Milan, 1954.

Il Mito di Prometeo e gli Ideali della Nuova Scienza (Rivista di Filosofia, vol. xLvi).

Francesco Bacone e la Tradizione Filosofica (Rendiconti Istituto Lombardo di Scienze e Lettere, vol. Lxxxviii).

Sulla Valutazione delle Arti Meccaniche nei Secoli XVI a XVII (Rivista critica di Storia della Filosofia, 1956).

Francesco Bacone: Dalla Magia alla Scienza. Bari, 1957.

I filosofi e le macchine (1400–1700). Milan, 1962.

Schweitzer, Albert, *Civilization and Ethics*. London, 1946.

Seebohm, F., *The Oxford Reformers of 1498*. London, 1867.

Shaw, Peter, *Francis Bacon methodized and made English*. London, 1733.

Spedding, Ellis and Heath, *The Works of Francis Bacon*. 14 vols, London, 1857–74.

Stephen, Robert, *Letters and Remains of the Lord Chancellor Bacon*. London, 1734. (First publication of *Redargutio Philosophiarum*.)

Tenison, E. M., *Elizabethan England*. Vol. ix. London, 1950.

Tenison, Archbishop T., *Baconiana*. London, 1679.

Trevelyan, G. M., *History of England*. London, 1943.

Trevor-Roper, H. R., *The General Crisis of the 17th Century* (Past and Present, No. 16, November 1959, pp. 31–64).

INDEX

Agricola, G., 33, 53
Agrippa, C., 19, 36, 52, 53, 70
Alchemy, 13, 51–3, 65–7, 74, 87, 122–3
Alexander the Great, 81, 107, 132
Ambition, various kinds of, 92–3
Anaxagoras, 68
Anderson, Fulton H., 16, 17, 18, 38, 48, 50, 57, 134
Andrewes, Lancelot, 26, 46, 47, 134
Aquinas, Thomas, 19, 64
Aristotle, 19, 42, 63, 71, 83, 84, 86, 89, 111, 112–15, 129, 130
Art of discovery advances with progress of discovery, 101–2
Aubrey, Aubrey's Lives, 11, 125 (note), 134
Authorised Version, 25
Avicebron, 84 (note)

Bacon, Francis
  List of writings, 1603–9, 11
  Hopes to effect reform administratively, 12
  Becomes M.P., 13
  Writes Temporis Partus Maximus, 13
  Offends the Queen, 14
  Friendship with Essex, 14–15
  First publications, Essays and Sacred Meditations, 16, 30, 31
  Influenced by English Reformation, 17
  Writes Temporis Partus Masculus, 17–20, 35–7
  Doctrine of Idols, 19, 39–40, 72
  Bible v. Aristotle, 21–6
  Dominion over nature, 27–9
  Attitude to manual arts, 32–4, 97
  Writes Valerius Terminus, 38–40
  Doctrine of Signs, 40, 103, 109, 112, 123, 125, 126, 127, 128
  Writes De Rerum Natura, 40–1
  Writes De Scientia Humana, 40–3
  Publishes Advancement of Learning, 43–4
  Writes Cogitata et Visa, 45–6
  Writes Redargutio Philosophiarum, 45–6
  Plans for headship of some college, 47
  Publishes De Sapientia Veterum, 48–50, 82 (note), 86–7, 120–1

Bacon, Roger, 22, 52
Bacon, Sir Nicholas, 12
Blackbourne, John, 34, 134
Boccaccio, 48
Bodin, Jean, 34, 134
Bruno, Giordano, 27, 78 (note)
Burleigh, Lord, 11, 30
Bushell, Thomas, 15, 34

Calvin, 17
Campanella, 78 (note)
Campbell, W. E., 17, 134
Cardan, Jerome, 52, 63, 76 (note), 85
Caspari, F., 17, 35, 134
Cave, William, 23, 134
Cecil, Lord, 38
Celsus, 68 (note), 125
Cicero, M. T., 28, 64
Colet, John, 17, 35
Conti, N., 48, 49 (note), 134
Crombie, A. C., 21, 22, 134
Curtis, Mark E., 12, 134

Democritus, 48, 68, 71, 80, 113
Dick, O. L., 125 (note), 134
Digges, Thomas, 129 (note)

Elizabeth, Queen, 11–15, 33, 38
Empedocles, 48, 68
Epicurus, 65, 71
Erasmus, 17, 33
Essex, Lord, 14
Experientia literata, 99, 119 (note)

Ficino, Marsilio, 35, 78 (note)
Finch, Sir John, 25
Florio, Michael Angelo, 33
Fontana, Domenico, 128 (note)
Fracastor, 85

Galen, 19, 64
Galileo, 78 (note)

Gardiner, S., 35, 134
Gilbert, Sir Humphrey, 12–13, 35, 134
Gilbert, Wm., 85
Glass, 97
Gunpowder, 71, 96, 97

Harvey, Wm., 115 (note)
Hatch, Edwin, 23, 134
Hebrew studies, 25
Heraclitus, 42, 68, 70
Herbert, George, 54
Hippocrates, 19, 67

Idols, doctrine of, 19, 39–40, 72
Induction, 83, 88–90
Inventions, philosophy of, 90, 93, 96

uvenal, 113

Laertius, Diogenes, 108 (note)
Lagarde, A., 17, 134
Leibnitz, 43
Lipschutz, A., 51, 134
Livy, 132 (note)
Lucan, 107 (note)
Lucretius, 116
Luther, 17

Machiavelli, 31
Magic, 51, 74, 88, 123
Maritain, J., 21, 135
Matthew, Toby, 24, 46
Mechanical arts,
    Importance for natural history, 42–3
    Limitations of, 74
    Inherent progress of, 97
Medical practitioners, 73
Method, equalizes wits, 118, 119 (note)
Mondolfo, R., 27, 135

Natural philosophy neglected, 76
Nef, John U., 13, 135
Neoplatonism, 84 (note)
Neoscholasticism, 21

Obelisk, raising of, 128–9
Organisation of learning defective, 79
Ovid, 28, 123 (note)

Pagel, W., 36, 115, 135
Palissy, B., 33, 53, 135
Paracelsus, 19, 36, 52, 65–7, 71
Parry, E. St John, 17, 135
Philosophy, traditional, defects of, 73, 106 ff.,
    111
Plato, 19, 35, 64, 71, 83, 115
Platt, Sir Hugh, 14
Pliny the Elder, 123 (note)
Plutarch, 64, 114 (note), 125 (note)
Presocratics, Bacon's interest in, 68, 84, 111
    (note), 116
Printing, 95, 97
Pythagoras, 68, 84

Ramus, Peter, 17, 19, 36, 39, 63–4
Rawley, Dr., 30
Read, Conyers, 14, 135
Rossi, Manlio, 11
Rossi, Paolo, 8, 11, 21, 33, 35, 36, 48, 49, 57,
    135

Scholasticism, 13, 19, 24, 118
Schweitzer, A., 29, 135
Scotus, Duns, 19
Scriptural quotations, 23, 79 (note), 92, 109
    (note), 112 (note), 113, 125 (note), 131
    (note), 132 (note)
Seebohm, F., 17, 135
Selden, John, 25
Seneca, 64
Severinus, Peter, 18, 57, 66, 71
Signs, Bacon's doctrine of, 40, 103, 109, 112,
    123, 125, 126, 127, 128
Silk-worm, 96
Singer, D. W., 27, 28, 135
Solomon, King, 92
Spedding, J., 11, 12
Stage-plays, false philosophies compared to,
    19, 62, 69, 84, 85, 116, 117
Sugar, 97

Tacitus, 31, 71–2
Telesius, B., 69, 85, 117

Tenison, Archbishop, 32, 49

Tenison, E. M., 15, 135

Theology, foe to natural philosophy, 77, 78

Theory and practice, divorce between, 97–8

Trevelyan, G. M., 25, 135

Trevor-Roper, H. R., 35 (note), 135

Tyndale, Wm., 25

Vergil, 124 (note)

Wycliffe, 24

Xenophon, 110

Zwingli, 25